PhotoPlus X3 User Guide

How to Contact Us

Our main office (UK, Europe):	The Software Centre PO Box 2000, Nottingham, NG11 7GW, UK
Main:	(0115) 914 2000
Registration (UK only):	(0800) 376 1989
Sales (UK only):	(0800) 376 7070
Customer Service/ Technical Support:	http://www.serif.com/support
General Fax:	(0115) 914 2020
North American office (USA, Canada):	The Software Center 13 Columbia Drive, Suite 5, Amherst NH 03031, USA
Main:	(603) 889-8650
Registration:	(800) 794-6876
Sales:	(800) 55-SERIF or 557-3743
Customer Service/ Technical Support:	http://www.serif.com/support
General Fax:	(603) 889-1127

Online

Visit us on the web at: http://www.serif.com/

International

Please contact your local distributor/dealer. For further details, please contact us at one of our phone numbers above.

Credits

Contents

1
Welcome

Welcome to **PhotoPlus** X3 from **Serif**—more than ever, the best value in image creation and editing software for any home, school, organization, or growing business. PhotoPlus is the number one choice for working with photographs and paint-type images, whether for the Web, multimedia, or the printed page.

PhotoPlus has the features you'll need... from importing or creating pictures, through manipulating colours, making image adjustments, applying filter effects and so much more, all the way to final export. Built-in support for the most modern digital cameras makes it easy to open your very own digital photos, either as JPG or as unprocessed raw images.

PhotoPlus also offers on-computer post-shoot development, using **Raw Studio**, where you're in full control of your raw image's white balance, exposure, and more.. as well as perform "blown" highlight recovery. Raw Studio complements other studios, such as **QuickFix Studio**, **Filter Gallery**, and **Instant Artist** for respective image correction, filter effects, and stunning artistic effects.

For an overview of PhotoPlus, see Existing features and New features (specific to PhotoPlus X3).

Don't forget to register your new copy, using the **Registration Wizard** on the **Help** menu. That way, we can keep you informed of new developments and future upgrades!

New features

- **16- bit Colour Depth/Detail** (p. 27)
  Work to high levels of detail (16-bits/channel) in both RGB and greyscale modes. Each mode can be adopted from scratch or after raw/HD photo import and when outputting HDR merge results.

- **Post-shoot Raw "Development" with Raw Studio** (p. 21)
  Open raw files in Raw Studio and fine tune your work with **white balance**, **exposure**, **noise reduction**, and **chromatic aberration** adjustments. Recover "blown" image highlights with the fantastic **Highlight recovery** feature. A supporting multi-colour histogram aids exposure and recovery control.

Effects and Adjustments

- **New Effect Filters!** (p. 123)
  Make a creative difference to your project with **Shear** and **Kaleidoscope** effects. Simulate traditional film with the **Film Grain** effect. Alternatively, simulate an elegant **Page Curl**, or whip up a storm with the cloud-like **Plasma** filter.

- **Merge Bracketed Photos** (p. 127)
  Use **HDR (High Dynamic Range) Merge** to bring together same-shot photos, each taken at different exposure settings. The composite photo, of wider dynamic range, would otherwise be impossible to capture in one shot. Optionally save intermediate HDR images for future use.

- **New Stunning 3D Layer Effects** (p. 118)
  3D effects are boosted with **Reflection Maps**—use bitmaps of indoor/outdoor environments to map onto your layer objects. PhotoPlus also now offers **transparency** control to create realistic glass-like reflective surfaces. Multiple separately coloured lights can also be added for dramatic **lighting effects**.

- **Noise Reduction** (p. 123)
  Photos showing speckles and blotches? Avoid noise from low-light conditions or when using high ISO settings with **Noise Reduction** as a separate effect or within QuickFix Studio.

- **Black and White Studio**
  Create stunning black and white compositions through a series of automated commands in the How To tab. Simply click on the images and tools and the effect is applied automatically to your image.

Import/Export

- **Import and Export HD Photos** (p. 199)
  Import Microsoft's new high-definition image file format. **Export Optimizer** will now export to HD photo and TIF from any PhotoPlus Picture; even to 48- and 64-bit RGB (or 16-bit Greyscale).

Printing

- **Print Studio** (p. 191)

  PhotoPlus's new unified **Print Studio** allows you to print single
  images, artistic and paper-saving layouts as well as contact sheets. Use
  the large range of built in layouts or quickly and easily create your
  own.

Correction

- **Enhanced QuickFix Studio** (p. 108)

  Enjoy the new **Noise Reduction** and **HSL
  (Hue/Saturation/Lightness)** adjustments; **Exposure** control and
  Black and White Film adjustments are new improvements. A
  Histogram pane shows your colour channels—really useful when
  adjusting white balance and brightness/contrast!

..and some other enhancements you've requested

- **More QuickShapes** and equivalent selection tools—now use triangle,
  cross, and speech callout shapes. The Colour tab now hosts an **HSL
  colour wheel** and HSL colour box. Read **IPTC metadata** and
  unlimited EXIF information from any photo.

Existing features

Document power

- **Professional Input and Output Options**

  Import an impressive selection of graphic files, including raw images
  from all the major manufacturers' cameras (and many more...).
  Support for Photoshop® (.PSD) and Corel Paint Shop Pro® import!
  Export to an equally extensive choice of graphic file formats!

- **Preset Canvas Sizes**

  If you're creating a new picture, adopt a preset **canvas size** selected
  from Photo, Video, Web, Animation or International/US Paper
  categories. Alternatively, create your own categories and canvas sizes
  which can be saved for future use!

- **Histogram Support**

  The Histogram tab dynamically responds to show the values for the currently active selection within your document. See how curves and level adjustments affect your image as they happen!

- **Versatile Layer Management**

  Create **standard** layers of varying opacity over your **Background** layer. Select, link, merge, arrange, hide, duplicate one or multiple layers all at the same time. Grouping of layers offers easier "bulk" manipulation and better organization. Blend Modes can be applied between layers. Shape and Text layers can be edited at any time; Adjustment and Filter layers offer non-destructive image correction and effects. **Masking** is supported on all layer types.

Essential Tools

- **Unique Selection Options**

  PhotoPlus goes well beyond the basic rectangle, ellipse, freehand, and polygon lasso tools, adding more than a dozen completely customizable selection shapes like polygons, spirals, and stars. Use Magnetic Selection to find edges as you trace them. Or define a selection shaped like text! Paint to Select mode lets you literally "brush on" selectedness. Store and load selections between any open file. Use combination buttons (as for shapes) to define cutout selection regions. Convert selections into paths.

- **Crop to Common Print Sizes**

  Use the Crop Tool for easy cropping to different portrait and landscape preset and custom print sizes—print resolution will auto-adjust to honour any print size.

- **Special Erase Options**
  Need to remove that blue sky and leave the clouds? Use the Flood Eraser to fill the blue regions with transparency. Want to isolate a shape from a flat colour background? The Background Eraser samples pixels under the brush, so only unwanted colours drop out.

- **Image cutouts**
  The Extract feature make short work of intelligently cutting out a subject from its background (or vice versa).

Colour

- **Channels**
  Use PhotoPlus's Channels tab to edit the Red, Green and Blue channels independently.

- **Custom and preset colour selection**
  The Colour tab operates in RGB, CMYK, HSL, and Greyscale models for selecting foreground and background colours when painting, creating lines or filling shapes. Use the Swatches tab for themed galleries of preset colour swatches. Use a Web-browser safe category when outputting to the web.

- **Gradient Fills**
  Take your pick of radial, linear, conical, or square fills—perfect for masking, to hide or reveal parts of your photo using smooth graduated blends to transparency. One **master dialog** allows editing of five gradient fill types combining both colour and transparency. Choose from a built-in gallery of presets, add your own categories and fills. (Of course, there's standard flood fill as well.)

- **Professional Colour Management**
  ICC colour profiling means you'll achieve more accurate colours with specific monitors and printers—for printed output that more closely matches on-screen colours.

Brushes, lines and shapes

- **Brushes**
  The **Paintbrush Tool** lets you apply brush strokes using preset brush tips.. choose a tip from basic, calligraphic, and various media categories (watercolour, charcoal, paint, etc.). Stamp and Spray Picture Brush effects and stamps . PhotoPlus lets you create your own category and brush tips! Apply different colours, levels of transparency, blend modes, to any brush, all at varying flow rates. Built-in support for most pressure-sensitive graphics tablets.

- **Freehand and Bézier Curve and Shape Drawing**
  Powerful vector-drawing tools let you produce any shape under the sun with controllable, connectable, editable line segments.

- **Editable QuickShapes**
  Easy to create, easy to change! Simply drag sliders to morph chevrons, hearts, badges, teardrops, moons, zigzags, and many more... apply layer effects and gradient fills... and edit any shape at any time. Create multiple shapes on a single layer—add, subtract, intersect, or exclude with previous shapes for frames, cutouts and custom contours. Draw directly as a Shape layer, path or as a filled bitmap on a raster layer.

- **Paths**
  Use the full range of line- and shape-drawing tools to create editable outlines via the **Paths tab**. Convert paths to or from selections on any layer. "Stroke" paths using any brush to create bordered shapes!

Text

- **Editable Text**
  Add formatted colour text directly onto your image, reposition and scale it by dragging. Text layers keep the contents separate so you can go back and edit selected areas of text or adjust formatting (colour, transparency, etc.) at any time!

Effects

- **Filter Gallery**
  The distort, blur, edge, sharpen, render and distortion effects can be applied singularly or in combination within a **Filter Gallery**... guaranteed to keep you up late!

- **Filter Layers**
  Convert to Filter Layer creates a non-destructive layer for powerful control of applied filter effects—switch filter effects on/ off, modify or add to an existing set of filter effects at a later date. Apply to standard or Background layers. For either, your layer content now remains unaffected!

- **Special Effects**
  A wild and whimsical assortment for instant creativity! **Instant Artist** effects turn your photos into works of art. PhotoPlus supports third-party Photoshop® plug-ins, and even lets you design your own custom filters.

- **Layer Effects**
  Add 2D Layer Effects such as **Shadow**, **Glow**, **Bevel**, **Outline** and **Emboss** for a sophisticated look on text or other image elements. Apply multiple effects onto a layer's existing effects for stunning design output. Move into the realm of astounding 3D Lighting and Surface Effects—advanced algorithms bring flat shapes to life! Vary surface and source **light properties**. Start with a pattern or a function, adjust parameters for incredible **surface contours, textures, fills**. Try 3D Painting using Depth Maps to add **instant dimensionality** to your artwork. Painting or erasing on a layer's depth map appears as raised or lowered strokes on the image! Use with 3D layer effects to achieve "carved" side-view textures.

- **Versatile Deform and Warp Tools**
  The "Swiss Army Knife" of image tools, the **Deform Tool** lets you rotate, resize, skew, reshape, or add perspective to any selection or layer. Warp tools pull, stretch, and distort image details, or shrink and enlarge. Pixels turn to putty with the **Mesh Warp Tool**!

Adjustments

- **Image Adjustments**
  Apply professional, darkroom-style colour and histogram adjustments to your images—giving you fingertip control over tones and colours. Adjust Shadow/Highlight/Midtone to calm down overexposed skies in one single operation without having to resort to manipulating curves and levels. Employ the **Blur** and **Sharpen** tools to enhance or reduce local detail... blend multiple layers more cleanly. There's even a dedicated tool for removing "red eye" from flash photos.

- **Editable Adjustment Layers**
  Not only apply colour corrections and special effects, but store each change on a separate layer or group. To fine-tune any adjustment later, just click its layer and change the settings! The Instant Effects gallery puts 3D technology and layer effects at your disposal.

- **QuickFix Studio**
  Use for cumulative image adjustments to **White Balance**, **Brightness&Contrast**, as well as **Straighten** and **Crop** your images. Equally, apply a **Black and White Film** effect, **Sharpen**, and fix **Red Eye** and various lens-related problems amongst many others. A full-screen dual-image preview display lets you compare and fix your images in an instant.

- **Retouching**
  Clone, Smudge, and Erase tools are included as essential retouch tools. Use the QuickFix Studio's **Blemish Remover** to subtly remove skin blemishes and unwanted light reflections—all via blending. For more heavy-duty retouch work, use the **Patch Tool** which is especially good for blending out irregularly-shaped regions!

Productivity/Workflow

- **Always-at-Hand Tools**
  A **Context toolbar** improves your efficiency by allowing the viewing and editing of a tool's properties in context with the tool currently selected; save and retrieve your favourite tool settings via a Tool Presets tab.

- **Macros**

  Macros let you automate your actions by using a huge number of categorized macro presets—alternatively, record and apply your own macro to any number of photos—give all your photos the same frame, age them or make a colour enhancement all at the same time!

- **Batch Processing**

  Use batch processing to repeat your tasks, e.g. changing file types, all at the same time without user intervention. When used in conjunction with macros the possibilities are endless.

Web and Animation

- **Image Slicing and Image Maps**

  Now it's not just the pros who can use these techniques to add links to Web graphics! Simply click to divide images into segments—each with its own hyperlink and popup text—or add hotspots to specific regions. PhotoPlus outputs the HTML code and lets you preview the results directly in your Web browser.

- **Animation Tools**

  It's easy and fun to create or edit animations for the Web. You can import and export animated GIFs, apply special effects (including 2D and 3D), tweening, even let PhotoPlus create entire animations for you automatically. Or export to the .AVI format for movies and multimedia! **Convert to Animation** makes the process of taking any image into animation mode a breeze!

Print and Share

- **Easy Printing**

  Print your project with powerful scaling and tiling options.

- **Publish to PDF**

  Export your documents to PDF, with powerful options for professional printing (PDF/X-1 compatibility and prepress marks).

- **Powerful Image Export Optimizer**
  The Export Optimizer lets you see how your image will look (and how much space it will take up) *before* you save it! Its multi-window display provides side-by-side WYSIWYG previews of image quality at various output settings, so you can make the best choice every time.

Installation

If you need help installing Windows, or setting up peripherals, see Windows documentation and help.

System Requirements

Minimum:

- Pentium PC with DVD/CD drive and mouse

- Microsoft Windows® XP or Vista operating system

- 128MB RAM

- 328MB (recommended install) free hard disk space

- SVGA display (800x600 resolution, 16-bit colour or higher)

Additional disk resources and memory are required when editing large and/or complex images.

Optional:

- Windows-compatible printer

- TWAIN-compatible scanner and/or digital camera

- Stylus or other input device, including pressure-sensitive pen

- Internet account and connection required for accessing online resources

First-time install

To install Serif PhotoPlus X3, simply insert your Program CD into your
DVD/CD drive. If AutoPlay is enabled on the drive, this automatically starts the
Setup Wizard. If you are installing PhotoPlus on Microsoft Windows® Vista, you
may need to click on **Run autorun.exe** from within the **Autoplay** dialog. If
AutoPlay is not enabled (or doesn't start the install automatically), use the
Manual install method described below.

1. From the initial screen, you'll be prompted to install **PhotoPlus X3**.

2. The Setup Wizard begins with a **Welcome** dialog, click **Next>**.

3. To add customer information, enter your **User Name**, **Organization**
   (if applicable), and your software **Product Key**.

   For product key information, click ⌨. Click **Next>**.

4. Please read through the scrollable license agreement, then if you agree
   to the terms, enable the **I Accept...** button. Click **Next>**.

5. Choose a US or UK language for your install. Click **Next>**.

6. (Optional) Check file types you would like to be associated with
   PhotoPlus. Click **Next>**.

7. Choose Setup Options using the tree menu to control which features
   are installed. Pick **Change...** for a different install location if needed.

8. Choose Shortcut Options for Start Menu program group, Desktop,
   and Quick Launch. Click **Next>**.

9. From the **Ready to Install** screen, click **Install**.

10. The dialog will display a progress bar as the program installs.
    Installation is completed after you click the **Finish** button.

Your installation is now complete and you can begin using Serif PhotoPlus X3!

Manual install

For manual installation, use My Computer (Windows® XP), or Computer
(Windows® Vista), to navigate to the DVD/CD drive in which your PhotoPlus
Program CD is located. Double-click the CD's icon and then double-click
setup.exe in the displayed folder. Choose Serif PhotoPlus X3 from the dialog,
then follow the on-screen installation instructions as described above.

2
Getting Started

Startup Wizard

Once PhotoPlus has been installed, you're ready to start!

- The Setup routine during install adds a **Serif PhotoPlus X3** entry to the Windows Start menu. Use the Windows **Start** button to pop up the Start Menu, click on **All Programs** and then click the PhotoPlus item.

On program launch, the Startup Wizard is displayed which offers different routes into PhotoPlus:

If you don't want to use the Startup Wizard again, check the "Don't show this wizard again" box. However, we suggest you leave it unchecked until you're familiar with the equivalent PhotoPlus commands. Switch the wizard back on again by checking **Use Startup Wizard** via **Preferences...** (General menu option) on the **File** menu.

Starting from scratch

PhotoPlus deals with two basic kinds of image files. We'll differentiate them as **pictures** (still images) and **animations** (moving images). The two types are closely related, and creating either from scratch in PhotoPlus involves the same series of steps.

PhotoPlus lets you create an image based on a pre-defined canvas size (e.g., 10 x 8 in). Different canvas size options are available from a range of categories (International/US Paper, Photo, Video, Web, or Animation). Alternatively, you can create your own custom canvas sizes, and even store them for future use. For either preset or custom sizes, the resolution can be set independently of canvas size.

When you create a new picture, you can choose to work in different colour modes, i.e. RGB or Greyscale, in either 8- or 16-bits/channel. Use a **Bit Depth** of 16 bit for higher levels of image detail modes.

To create a new picture or animation (using Startup Wizard):

1. The first time you launch PhotoPlus, you'll see the **Startup Wizard**, with a menu of choices. Click **Create>New Image** or **Create>New Animation**.

2. In the New Image dialog, you can either:

    1. For a **preset** canvas size, select a suitable **Category** from the drop-down list. Categories are named according to how your image or animation is intended to be used, e.g. pick a Photo category for photo-sized canvases.

    2. Pick a canvas **Size** from the drop-down list.

    OR

    -   For a custom canvas size, enter your own **Width** and **Height**. If the dimensions are non-standard, the Size drop-down list will be shown as "Custom." For future use, save the custom size with **Add Size...** (from the ▽ button) if necessary.

> Although you can resize the image canvas size (width x height) later, it's usually best to allow some extra canvas area at first.

3. Add a **Resolution** for the new image file. Leave the resolution at 96.00 pixels/inch unless you're sure a different value is required.

4. Select a **Colour Mode**, choosing to operate in RGB or Greyscale mode.

5. (Optional) Select a **Bit Depth** of 16 bits per channel for projects which require higher levels of colour detail. Otherwise a bit depth of 8 bits/channel is used as default.

6. Select a background type in the **Background** drop-down list.
   • When painting a picture from scratch, you'll normally choose White.
   • You can also choose Background Colour, to use the current background colour shown on the Colour tab.
   • When creating an animation, Transparent is often called for.

7. When you've made your selections, click **OK.**

To create a new picture or animation (during your session):

1. If the Startup Wizard is disabled, click [icon] **New** on the **Standard** toolbar.

2. In the New Image dialog, set your canvas size (see above) and then check **Animation** to create an animation or leave unchecked for a picture.

3. Click **OK**. The new image or animation opens in a separate untitled window.

Opening an existing file

You can use the Startup Wizard to access image files recently viewed in PhotoPlus or open any image file. PhotoPlus opens all the standard image formats for print and web graphics, in addition to its native .SPP format and Adobe Photoshop .PSD files.

Raw files open in a **Raw Studio** environment, which offers image adjustment on the "undeveloped" image before opening. See Opening a raw image on p. 21. Similarly, intermediate HDR images (OpenEXR and Radiance) can be opened in a dialog at any time for readjusting your HDR merge results.

To open a saved image file (via Startup Wizard):

1. From the Startup Wizard (at startup time or via **File>New...**), click **Open>Saved Work**. You'll see a list of recently opened files. To see a preview of any file, click its name in the list.

2. To open a selected file, click **Finish**.

    OR

1. Click **Browse** to locate other saved files. To narrow or expand the list of file types shown in the Open dialog, select from the lower-right drop-down list.

2. Select the folder and file name and click the **Open** button.

PhotoPlus opens the image as a maximized currently active document; the document appears in the Documents tab.

> 🔖 Recently viewed files also appear at the bottom of the **File** menu. Simply select the file name to open it.

To open any image file:

1. From the Startup Wizard (at startup time or via **File>New...**), click **Open>Image Browser**.
   OR

   Click the 🔲 **Open** button on the **Standard** toolbar.

2. In the Open dialog, select the folder and file name. To open multiple files, press the **Ctrl** or **Shift** key when selecting their names.

3. Click the **Open** button to open the desired image as a maximized document.

To open images by drag-and-drop:

- Drag and drop an image file or preview thumbnail into PhotoPlus from Windows Explorer either:

  - into the current workspace (to create a new layer).
    OR

  - onto the Documents tab (to create a new image window).

Opening a raw image

High-specification SLR digital cameras give the option of saving your photos as JPG, and more recently, as raw files. On some cameras, you may have the best of both worlds, by saving as both simultaneously.

Quite why you would choose one format over the other depends on a host of factors, such as the type of workflow and the level of detail you want to work to. This is best summarized in the following table.

JPG	raw
Basic level of colour or greyscale detail, inherently 8-bit images.	**Highest** level of colour or greyscale detail, inherently 16-bit images.
Smaller file sizes (so more files per memory card with a faster write-to-card time)	**Larger** file sizes (so less files per memory card and a longer write time)
JPG files are **automatically processed** by camera	raw files are **unprocessed** by camera
Limited adjustment control (post-shoot)	**Absolute** adjustment control (post-shoot)

There is a healthy debate in the photographic industry about which format to choose. Professionally, the old idiom "horses for courses" applies. For example, the need for fast shoot-to-print time (using JPGs) is essential for sports photographers where post-shoot adjustment is not practical. Conversely, a wedding photographer may wish to work with the maximum amount of colour information (using raw images) and then typically make post-shoot adjustments, maintaining flexibility and a high detail throughout.

For the amateur or semi-professional photographer, the same factors apply, but format choice may be governed more by quality expectations or cost, rather than "workflow" issues.

Workflow refers to the shoot-to-print progress when working with JPG or raw files. A JPG workflow is destructive, in that your JPG file is "developed" in your camera without user intervention. Conversely, a raw workflow is non-destructive because your raw file is "undeveloped"—you can control your image's development within your photo-editing program (PhotoPlus).

PhotoPlus's **Raw Studio** offers post-shoot adjustments to any raw file **without** affecting the original file. **White balance**, **exposure**, **highlight recovery**, **noise reduction**, and the removal of **chromatic aberration** are all possible. With an in-built histogram, it's easy to firstly check exposure levels and to spot any highlight clipping (suggesting image overexposure), and to secondly make adjustments using the human eye and the histogram in combination.

Once you click **OK** you won't be able to undo your adjustments—it's therefore recommended to spend time "developing" your image correctly before exiting Raw Studio.

Once you've exited Raw Studio you'll enter the usual PhotoPlus user interface. As for any other file format you can then optionally add text, lines, shapes, and apply some creative filter effects (not all effects are available in 16 bits/channel mode). On saving (**File>Save** or **File>Save As...**), you'll be prompted to save your work as a PhotoPlus picture (.SPP) only. Typically most users would then export to a 16-bit file format such as .TIF or .HDP.

To adjust a raw image:

1. Open a raw file by using **Open** on the **Standard** toolbar. (see Starting from scratch on p. 18). If opening multiple raw files, once you've adjusted an image, Raw Studio will load the next image automatically until all files are loaded.

   > Open raw images previously copied to your computer, rather than directly from your camera's memory card (e.g., SD).

2. From Raw Studio, adopt the program's, camera's or a custom white balance.

   - **Auto**: White balance calculated automatically by PhotoPlus. The camera's white balance setting is ignored.

   - **Camera**: The camera's manual or automatic white balance setting is used. PhotoPlus is not used to set white balance.

   - **Custom**: Click **Colour Selector** then hover over a neutral colour on the screen to calculate the white balance manually. Typically, a subject's white shirt or blue sky can be clicked on as the neutral "reference"point.

3. Drag the **Exposure** slider left or right to make the image darker or lighter. The values are equivalent to your camera's f-stop settings, i.e. a value of 1 = 1 f-stop.

   > When increasing the Exposure value, use the histogram to check that your highlights aren't clipped (i.e., when the graph disappears abruptly off the right-hand edge of the histogram).

4. Drag the **Black Point** slider right to set the darkest parts of the image to black (by shifting the histogram's left-most edge, making all "clipped" pixels in the shadow region turn black).

5. For recovery of blown highlights, from the **Mode** drop-down menu choose **Recovery**, and if needed, increase the **Strength** slider until you get ideal results. The **Clip** option, as default, means that highlights remain blown (no recovery is attempted). The **Neutral** option also recovers highlights if you're experiencing colour casting.

6. For Noise reduction set a **Strength**. Noise may be evident on images captured in low light or with a high ISO camera setting. The greater the value, the more smoothing occurs to remove speckling. Too much noise reduction may produce an unwanted blurring effect.

7. Remove unwanted **Chromatic Aberration** (colour fringing on object edges on high-contrast photos) by adjusting **Red/Cyan** or **Blue/Yellow** sliders. Each slider adjusts one colour channel relative to the other channel.

8. To reduce the colour information down to "8 Bits/Channel", select from the **Bit Depth** option. By default, optimum raw colour information is preserved (i.e., 16 Bits/Channel). (See Colour modes for more details).

9. From the **Colour Space** drop-down menu, assign a colour space to your image which matches your intended colour **workspace**. For professional work, AdobeRGB, ProPhoto, or WideGamut offer larger colour spaces (i.e more colours) than the standard RGB (sRGB) space (this is acceptable for most users), but you'll need to enable colour management and pick the same colour space as your chosen workspace. (See online Help).

10. Click **OK** (or **Reset** to discard applied adjustments). The raw image becomes your PhotoPlus document.

Acquiring a TWAIN image

If your digital camera or scanner supports the industry-wide **TWAIN** standard, you can bring pictures from these devices directly into PhotoPlus.

To set up your TWAIN device for importing:

- See the documentation supplied with the device for operating instructions.

To import a TWAIN image:

1. (via Startup Wizard) Choose **Import From Twain**.
    OR
    (During your PhotoPlus session) Choose **Import** from the **File** menu,
    then select **Acquire**.

2. Complete the procedure using the acquisition dialog associated with
    the selected TWAIN source.

If you have more than one TWAIN-compatible device installed, you may need
to select which source you wish to scan with.

To select a different TWAIN source for scanning:

*   Choose **Import** from the **File** menu, then choose **Select Source** from
    the submenu.

See PhotoPlus help for some useful tips about scanning.

Saving a file

The process of **saving** differs depending on the type of file you are working on,
the file's current saved state and the file type you want to save.

PhotoPlus lets you work on (and save) one of several file types:

*   An open **PhotoPlus Picture** (.SPP) file is project-based and so
    preserves 'project' information (e.g., layers, masks, paths) when saving
    the file.

*   For a currently open **image** file you can edit and save the image back
    to its original format. However, if you've added layers, masks, or paths
    to your image you'll be prompted to optionally create a .SPP file to
    preserve 'project' information (otherwise it will be lost). If you choose
    not to create a .SPP file, the additional content is included in the now
    flattened image.

*   An intermediate **HDR** image can be saved, which stores the results of
    an HDR Photo Merge in a .HDR file for future use. See Merging
    bracketed photos on p. 127 for more information.

To save your PhotoPlus Picture:

- Click the [icon] **Save** button on the **Standard** toolbar.
  OR
  To save under a different path or base name, choose **Save As...** from the **File** menu. The window title bar is updated accordingly.

  ★ If the current window is untitled or non-native, the Save As dialog opens, and prompts for a .SPP file name based on the base name shown in the title bar.

The procedure for an altered image is slightly more complicated as PhotoPlus will assist you in deciding if you want to save or lose any added "project information" added to the original image.

To save your currently open image:

- If you've altered the background layer only and no layers, paths, or masks have been added, you can save (without prompt) the altered image to its current base name (shown in the window title bar) by choosing **Save...** from the **File** menu. Changes are included in the image.
  OR

- If you've added layers, paths, or masks to your image, when you click **Save...** (**File** menu) you'll be asked if you want to preserve the 'project' information.

- In the dialog, click **Yes** to save your project information (as an .SPP file).
  OR
  click **No** to save as a flattened image (i.e., without layers).

To revert an image file:

- Click **Revert** from the **File** menu. The last saved version of your image is displayed.

Closing files and exiting

To close a single image window (file):

- Choose **Close** from the **File** menu.
  OR

- Click the Close button on the window's title bar.

You'll be prompted to save changes made since the last save.

To close all image windows (files):

- Choose **Close All** from the **File** menu.

You'll be prompted to save changes made to any open image since the last save.

To close PhotoPlus:

- Choose **Exit** from the **File** menu.

For each open file, you'll be prompted to save changes made since the last save.

Colour modes

PhotoPlus operates in several **colour modes** to let you work in standard and higher levels of colour or tonal detail—these are 8-bits/channel RGB (or 8-bits/channel Greyscale) and the more detailed 16-bits/channel RGB (or 16-bits/channel Greyscale). Editing in 8 bits/channel mode will use 256 levels per colour channel, as opposed to 16-bits/channel, which uses 65,536 levels per channel.

As a rule of thumb, use 16-bit working for "as-your-eyes-see-it" image accuracy.

If you work with 16-bit images, you'll probably want to benefit from the optimum colour or tonal information throughout your project. In fact, 16-bits/channel colour mode is invoked **automatically** when:

- importing a raw image from PhotoPlus's Raw Studio.

- opening a 16-bit Microsoft HD photo.

PhotoPlus also lets you **manually** choose modes:

	Choose..	Then pick...
when creating a new image	**Start New Picture** (Startup Wizard) or **File>New**	Colour Mode: RGB or Greyscale Bit Depth: 8 or 16 bits per channel
at any time	**Image>Colour Mode**	Colour 8-Bits/channel mode Colour 16-Bits/channel mode Greyscale 8-Bits/channel mode Greyscale 16-Bits/channel mode
when outputting the results of an HDR Merge	**File>HDR Merge...**	Output 16-bits per channel

At some point, you may have no need to work at a high level of detail (16 bits/channel). In converting to 8-bit mode, you may want to opt for smaller file sizes or take advantage of a greater selection of filter effects.

To switch from 16-bits/channel to 8-bits/channel working:

- From the **Image** menu, select **Colour Mode**, and pick an 8-bits/channel option from the submenu.

Like most 16-bit photo editing programs, the choice of filter effects available is limited while in a 16-bits/channel mode.

To check which mode is currently set, the Title bar shows the mode after the file name, e.g. CRW_4832.CRW @ 20%,3088 x 2056, **RGB 16 Bits/Channel.**

3
Manipulating Images

Making a selection

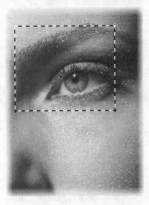

In any photo editing program, the **selection tools and techniques** are as significant as any of the basic brush tools or commands. The basic principle is simple: quite often you'll want to perform an operation on just a portion of the image. To do this you must define an active selection area.

The wide range of selection options in PhotoPlus lets you:

- Define just about any selection shape

- Modify the extent or properties of the selection (see p. 39)

- Carry out various manipulations on the selected pixels, including cut, copy, paste, rotate, adjust colours, apply special effects, etc. (see p. 43)

Selection basics

Although the techniques for using the various selection methods differ, the end result is always the same: a portion of the active layer has been "roped off" from the rest of the image. The boundary is visible as a broken line or **marquee** around the selected region.

Whenever there's a selection, certain tools and commands operate **only** on the pixels inside the selection—as opposed to a condition where nothing is selected, in which case those functions generally affect the entire active layer.

For example, when there's a selection, the brush tools only work inside the selection; the colour simply doesn't affect outside pixels.

The example opposite uses a freehand selection under the eye to keep the brush stroke within the selection area.

You can also apply an adjustment or special effect, affecting only the selected region.

You may occasionally (especially if the marquee is hidden) find yourself using a tool or command that seems to have no effect... it's probably because there's still a selection somewhere, and you're trying to work outside the selection. In this case, just cancel the selection.

- To cancel the selection (select nothing), right-click and choose **Deselect,** use the **Select** menu or press **Ctrl+D**.

The opposite of selecting nothing is selecting everything:

- To select the entire active layer, press **Ctrl+A**, or choose **Select All** from the **Select** menu.

For partial selection of opaque pixels, you can **Ctrl**-click the layer thumbnail (in Layers tab).

> If your image has multiple layers, and you switch to another layer, the selection doesn't stay on the previous layer—it follows you to the new active layer. This makes sense when you realize that the selection doesn't actually include image content—like an outline map, it just describes a region with boundaries.

Selection tool options

PhotoPlus offers a very wide range of other selection methods, and a variety of commands for modifying the extent or properties of the selected pixels—all available from the **Tools** toolbar. Note that the selection tools work on Background and standard layers, but not on text layers or shape layers.

The ▢▼ **Standard Selection Tools** flyout includes various tools which can be used to drag on the image to define a selection region.

- ▢ **Rectangle Selection Tool**—drag out a rectangular selection area of your chosen size (use the **Ctrl** key to constrain to a Square area).

- ◯ **Ellipse Selection Tool**—drag out an ellipse selection area (use **Ctrl** key to constrain to a circle).

- ◌ **Freehand Selection Tool**—lets you draw a freehand (irregular) line which is closed automatically to create an irregularly shaped selection area.

- ◌ **Polygon Selection Tool**—lets you draw a series of straight-line segments (double-click to close the polygon).

- ▣ **Magnetic Selection Tool**—lets you trace around an object edge creating a selection line that snaps to the edge as you drag.

The ▢▼ **Adjustable Selection Tools** flyout provides different variable shapes, including pie, star, arrow, heart, spiral, wave, and so on. Choose a tool, drag out a shape on the image, then adjust the handles to fine-tune the shape. Double-click within the shape to select the region.

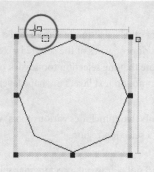

Here's how the adjustable selection tools work. We'll use the regular polygon selection shape as an example. Choose a tool from the flyout and drag out a shape on the image. You can hold down the **Ctrl** key to constrain the shape.

The regular polygon appears as an outline with two slider tracks bounding it. Each of the slider tracks has a square handle, and when you move the cursor on to the handle it will change to a + sign. As you drag a slider (circled above), the shape's properties change. In the case of the polygon, one slider varies the number of sides, while the other rotates the shape. Once you're satisfied with the selection, double-click in the centre (just as with the Crop Tool or Magnetic Selection Tool) to complete the marquee. The shape will then possess a dashed outline, becoming a selection.

The **Colour Selection Tool** lets you select a region based on the colour similarity of adjacent pixels—simply click a starting pixel then set a **Tolerance** from the context toolbar. It works much like the fill tool, but the result is a selected region rather than a region flooded with a colour.

For any selection tool, the Context toolbar includes combination buttons (**New**, **Add**, **Subtract**, and **Intersect**) that determine the effect of each new selection operation. For example, starting with a square selection (created with the **New** button), here's what a second partly overlaid square (shown with a solid line) might produce with each setting:

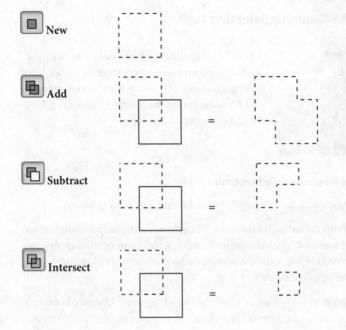

For Rectangle and Ellipse Selection tools, the Context toolbar additionally lets you set a **Fixed Size** or **Fixed Aspect**, or number of Rows or Columns (Rectangle Selection Tool only) in advance of creating your selection—great if you have a clear idea of the selection area required!

The **Text Selection Tool** lets you create a selection in the form of text. Click with the tool to display the Text cursor. Type your text, format as needed, and click **OK**.

Using the Magnetic Selection Tool

The  **Magnetic Selection Tool** makes it easy to isolate part of an image where there's already a bit of an edge showing. You simply trace around the edge, and PhotoPlus snaps the selection marquee to the nearest dramatic colour change.

To use the Magnetic Selection tool:

1. Click once on the image to place a starting node along an edge.

2. With the mouse button, trace along the edge; the marquee line follows the nearest edge. At regular distances, nodes automatically appear along the line. Only the portion of the line beyond the last node remains adjustable.

On the Context toolbar, you can adjust the tool's **Frequency** (distance between automatic nodes) and **Contrast** (edge sensitivity) for best results. As a shortcut, press the up and down arrow keys (or use your mouse's spinwheel) to adjust the contrast setting on the fly.

1. To add a node manually (for example, at a corner), click once.

2. To back up, press **Delete** to undo recent nodes one at a time; repeat as needed. To clear the marquee and start over, press **Esc**.

3. To temporarily switch to the Polygon selection tool, hold down the **Ctrl** key.

4. To close the selection region, double-click or click again on the starting node.

Colour Range

As an intelligent colour selection method, i.e. where selection is based on "tagging" a specific range of colours or tones in the image, choose the **Colour Range** command.

To select a colour range:

1. Choose **Colour Range...** from the **Select** menu. The Colour Range dialog appears, with the image visible in the Preview window.

2. To make an initial selection:

- To tag a particular colour or tone group, such as "Reds" or "Midtones," choose the group's name from the Select drop-down list.
  OR

  Click the [icon] **Colour Picker** button to reset the adjustment and then drag across a section of the image in the Preview window to tag a colour range. With this method, the **Tolerance** slider lets you include a wider or narrower range of colours in the selection.

[icons] Once you've made an initial selection, you can use the **Add Colour** and **Subtract Colour** buttons and drag to tweak the tagged range.

Meanwhile, the dialog provides visual feedback.

1. If **Show Selection** is checked, the greyscale Selection window on the right shows tagged values as brighter, with untagged pixels darker. To customize what's displayed in the Preview window on the left, choose an option from the Preview list: "None" shows the original image, "White Matte" shows tagged pixels through a white background, and so on.

2. Click **OK** to confirm the selection, or **Cancel** to abandon changes.

To create a selection based on the active layer's alpha (opacity) channel:

- **Ctrl**-click on the layer's image thumbnail.
  OR
  Choose **Create from Layer Alpha** from the **Select** menu.

This selects opaque portions of the image. Relatively more transparent areas become relatively less selected than opaque areas, i.e. more protected from changes.

Storing selections

Finally, you can **store selections** (i.e., just the marqueed region and per-pixel selectedness data) as part of either the current image or any open image file, and **load** a stored selection at any time. It's often useful to be able to "grab" the same region of an image at different phases of working on it. And, for repetitive tasks (preparing Web buttons, for example) on different but graphically similar files, by storing a selection you can reuse it rather than having to recreate it for each file.

Both **Store Selection...** and **Load Selection...** options are hosted on the right-click pop-up menu or **Select** menu (you can also delete any stored selection).

Modifying a selection

Once you've used a selection tool to select a region on the active layer, you can carry out a number of additional steps to fine-tune the selection before you actually apply an effect or manipulation to the selected pixels. Paint to Select mode even lets you use standard painting or editing tools as selection tools!

Transforming the selection

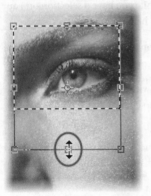

The **Selection Deform Tool** on the **Tools** toolbar's Deform Tools flyout lets you transform, scale or rotate any already drawn selection area. With the tool enabled, square nodes on the mid-points and corners of any selected area can be dragged (opposite).

Look for the cursor changing between resize and rotate modes when hovering over a corner node.

Use in conjunction with the **Ctrl** key to transform the selection area without constraint, creating a **skewed transform** (drag nodes as appropriate). The **Alt** key resizes the area about its centre, while the **Shift** key maintains the area's aspect ratio. It's also possible to move the small centre of rotation "handle" in the centre of the transform to produce an arc rotational movement rather than rotating around the area's centre (by default).

> Holding down the Shift key whilst rotating will cause a movement in 15 degree intervals.

Making the selection larger or smaller

If the selection you've made isn't quite the right shape, or doesn't quite include all the necessary pixels (or perhaps includes a few too many), you can continue to use the selection tools to add to, or subtract from, the selected region.

To add or subtract to/from the existing selection with a selection tool:

- Select the tool and drag while holding down the **Shift** or **Alt** key, respectively. The newly selected pixels don't have to adjoin the current selection—it's possible to select two or more separate regions on the active layer.

Modifying the selection

If you right-click (or choose the **Select** menu) while you have a selection on your page, a series of selection-related commands can be used:

- The **Invert** command selects the portion of the active layer outside the current selection. Unselected pixels become selected, and vice versa.

- The **Modify** item provides a submenu with several functions that can save you the trouble of hand-drawing to change the selection boundaries:

- Choose **Contract...** to shrink the borders of the selection, or **Expand...** to extend its borders. Each command displays a dialog that lets you enter a specific pixel value.

- Choose **Border...** to create a new selection as a "frame" of a specified pixel width around the current selection.

- **Grow** and **Similar** both expand the selection by seeking out pixels close (in colour terms) to those in the current selection. **Grow** only adds pixels adjacent to the current selection, while **Similar** extends the selection to any similar pixels in the active layer.
  Both commands use the tolerance setting entered for the Colour Selection Tool on the Context toolbar. As the tolerance increases, a larger region is selected. Typically when using these tools, you'll start by selecting a very small region (the particular colour you want to "find" in the rest of the image).

- If the selected region has ragged edges or discontinuous regions (for example, if you've just used the Colour Selection Tool), use the **Smooth...** command to even them out. The Radius setting determines the extent of smoothing.

Soft-edged and hard-edged selections

Antialiasing and **feathering** are different ways of controlling what happens at the edges of a selection. Both produce softer edges that result in smoother blending of elements that are being combined in the image. You can control either option for the Standard and Adjustable Selection tools, using the **Feather** input box (or slider) and **Antialias** check box on the Context toolbar.

- **Antialiasing** produces visibly smooth edges by making the selection's edge pixels semi-transparent. (As a layer option, it's not available on the Background layer, which doesn't support transparency.)

- If an antialiased selection (for example, one pasted from another image) includes partially opaque white or black edge pixels, you can use the **Matting** command on the **Layers** menu to remove these pixels from the edge region, yielding a smoother blend between the selection and the image content below. (Fully opaque edge pixels are not affected.)

- **Feathering** reduces the sharpness of a selection's edges, not by varying transparency, but by *partially selecting* edge pixels. If you lay down paint on a feathered selection, the paint will actually be less intense around the edges. You can apply feathering "after the fact" to an existing selection (but before applying any editing changes) using the **Select** menu's **Modify>Feather...** command. In the dialog, enter the width (in pixels) of the transition area. A higher value produces a wider, more gradual fade-out.

- **Threshold** converts a feathered, soft-edged selection into a hard-edged selection (use **Modify>Threshold**). As with feathering, you won't see an immediate effect on the image, but painting and other editing operations will work differently inside the selection.

Paint to Select mode

You can use **Paint to Select mode** (**Select** menu) to create a selection from scratch, or to modify an existing selection using standard painting and editing tools. In concept, it's similar to masking but in this case you're only adjusting what is selected on the layer, rather than the layer's bitmap (image) content.

In the illustration below, (**A**) depicts the incomplete selection on a white flower when using the Colour Selection Tool. In Paint to Select mode (**B**) the selected regions appear as a red colour mask (grey here). To make a selection of the entire flower, the remaining unselected regions are painted with a brush (with white as foreground colour), making a completely filled-in flower (**C**); switching off Paint to Select reveals the fully selected flower (**D**).

A   B   C   D

Manipulating a selection

Moving the selection marquee

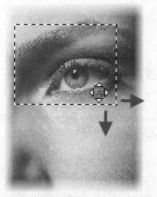

Sometimes, you need to adjust the position of the marquee without affecting the underlying pixels. Any time you're using one of the selection tools, the cursor over a selected region changes to the **Move Marquee** cursor, which lets you drag the marquee outline to reposition it.

You can also use the keyboard arrows to "nudge" the selection marquee. In this case you're only moving the selection outline—not the image content inside it.

Once you have selected your chosen pixels, the operations which can be performed include moving, cutting, copying, duplicating, pasting and deleting. You use the **Move Tool** to drag the selection *plus* its image content. (See Modifying a selection on p. 40).

Using the Move Tool

The **Move Tool** is for pushing actual pixels around. With it, you can drag the content of a selection from one place to another, rather than just moving the selection outline. To use it, simply click on the selection and drag to the new location. The selected part of the image moves also.

- If nothing is selected, dragging with the Move Tool moves the entire active layer. (Or, if the Move Tool's **Automatically select layer** property is selected on its context toolbar, the tool moves the first visible item's layer beneath the move cursor when you click to move.)

- When the Move Tool is chosen, you can also use the keyboard arrows to "nudge" the selection or active layer.

- The "hole" left behind when the image content is moved exposes the current background colour (on the Background layer), or transparency (see above; on standard layers), shown with a "checkerboard" pattern.

- To duplicate the contents of the selection on the active layer, press the **Alt** key and click, then drag with the Move Tool.

- As a shortcut if you're working with any one of the selection tools, you can press the **Ctrl** key to switch temporarily to the Move Tool. Press **Ctrl+Alt** to duplicate. Release the key(s) to revert to the selection tool.

Cut/Copy/Delete/Paste

Cut and copy operations on selections involving the Clipboard work just as in other Windows programs.

- To copy pixels in the selected region, press **Ctrl-C** or click the Copy button on the **Standard** toolbar. (You can also choose **Copy** from the **Edit** menu.)

- To cut the selected pixels, press **Ctrl-X** or choose **Cut** from the **Edit** menu.

- To delete the selected pixels, press the **Delete** key or choose **Clear** from the **Edit** menu.

Cut or deleted pixels expose the current background colour (on the Background layer) or transparency (on standard layers). If you want to create transparency on the Background layer, first "promote" it to a standard layer by right-clicking its name on the Layers tab and choosing Promote to Layer.

- If nothing is selected, a cut or copy operation affects the whole active layer, as if **Select All** were in effect.

When pasting from the Clipboard, PhotoPlus offers several options.

- To paste as a new image in an untitled window, press **Ctrl+V** or click the **Paste as New image** button on the **Standard** toolbar. (Or select from the **Edit>Paste** menu.)

- To paste as a new layer above the active layer, press **Ctrl+L** or choose **Paste> As New Layer** from the **Edit** menu.

- To paste into the current selection, press **Shift+Ctrl+L** or choose **Paste> Into Selection** from the **Edit** menu. The Clipboard contents appear centred in the currently selected region. (This choice is greyed out if there's no selection, or if the active layer is a text layer.) This option is useful if you're pasting from one layer to another. Because the selection marquee "follows" you to the new layer, you can use it to keep the pasted contents in registration with the previous layer.

- To duplicate part of the active layer on the same layer, press the **Alt** key and click, then drag with the Move Tool. (Or if you're working with a selection tool, press **Ctrl+Alt** and drag to duplicate.)

Changing image and canvas size

You probably know that image dimensions are given in **pixels** (think of pixels as the "dots of paint" that comprise a screen image)—say, 1024 wide by 768 high. If you want to change these dimensions, there are two ways to go about it, and that's where **image** and **canvas** come into play.

Changing the **image size** (top example opposite) means scaling the whole image (or just a selected region) up or down. Resizing is actually a kind of distortion because the image content is being stretched or squashed.

Changing the **canvas size** (bottom example) just involves adding or taking away pixels around the edges of the image. It's like adding to the neutral border around a mounted photo, or taking a pair of scissors and cropping the photo to a smaller size. In either case, the remaining image pixels are undisturbed so there's no distortion.

Note that once you've changed either the image size or the canvas size, the image and canvas are exactly the same size again!

Changing image size

The **Image Size** dialog lets you specify a new size for the whole image, in terms of its screen dimensions and/or printed dimensions.

To resize the whole image:

1.   Choose **Image Size...** from the **Image** menu.

2.   To specify just the printed dimensions, uncheck **Resize layers**. Check the box to link the Pixel Size (screen) settings to the Print Size or Resolution settings.

3.   To retain the current image proportions, check **Maintain aspect ratio**. Uncheck the box to alter the dimensions independently.

4.   If adjusting screen dimensions:

- Select a preferred scale (either "Pixels" or "Percent") in the drop-down list.

- Select a resampling method. As a rule, use Nearest Pixel for hard-edge images, Bilinear Interpolation when shrinking photos, Bicubic Interpolation when enlarging photos, and Lanczos3 Window when best quality results are expected.

5. If adjusting printed dimensions, select your preferred units of measurement and resolution. The pixel size will automatically alter with print size adjustment.

6. Enter the new values and click **OK**.

Changing canvas size

PhotoPlus provides several ways of changing the canvas size that was originally chosen when creating a new image (see p. 18). If you just want to reduce the canvas area, you can use the **Crop Tool** (see Cropping an image on p. 48) or the **Image>Crop to Selection** command. To either enlarge or reduce the canvas, the **Image>Canvas Size...** command provides a dialog that lets you specify where pixels should be added or subtracted.

To change canvas size:

1. Choose **Canvas Size...** from the **Image** menu.

2. Enter **New Width** and/or **New Height** values (the current values are also shown for comparison). Alternatively, select the **Relative** check box to enter the number of units you want to add or subtract from the existing width and height values—for example, 5 pixels, 1 cm, 100 points, 10 percent, and so on.

3. In the Anchor box, click to position the image thumbnail with respect to edges where pixels should be added or subtracted. For example, if you want to extend the canvas from all sides of the image, click the centre anchor point.

4. Click **OK**.

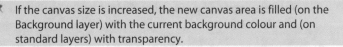

> ★ If the canvas size is increased, the new canvas area is filled (on the Background layer) with the current background colour and (on standard layers) with transparency.

Cropping an image

Cropping is the electronic equivalent of taking a pair of scissors to a photograph, except of course with a pair of scissors there is no second chance! Cropping deletes all of the pixels outside the crop selection area, and then resizes the image canvas so that only the area inside the crop selection remains. Use it to focus on an area of interest—either for practical reasons or to improve photo composition.

Before

After
(Rectangular Crop)

PhotoPlus allows you to crop unconstrained, or to a standard or custom print size.

To crop unconstrained:

1. Select the 📐 **Crop Tool** from the **Tools** toolbar's Crop Tools flyout. Ensure the **Unconstrained** option is set in the Context toolbar's first drop-down list.

2. Drag out a rectangle to create an unconstrained rectangle, then fine-tune the areas dimensions if needed by dragging the edges. Note that you can also constrain the crop area to be a square, by holding down the **Ctrl** key while dragging.

3. To crop to the designated size, double-click inside the crop area.

The **Shading** check box and **Opacity** option on the Context toolbar sets the shade colour and transparency of the unwanted region outside the rectangle, respectively. Uncheck Shading to view only the rectangle, with no shading and full transparency.

> Cropping with the Crop Tool affects all image layers. Everything outside the designated region is eliminated. If there's a marquee-based selection, it is ignored and deselected during cropping.

To crop to a specific print size or resolution:

1. Select the ⬜ **Crop Tool** from the **Tools** toolbar.

2. Then either:

   - For print sizes, choose a **pre-defined** print size (expressed in inches) from the first drop-down menu in the Context toolbar. Both portrait and landscape crop regions can be selected—e.g., 4 x 6 in for portrait, 6 x 4 in for landscape).
   OR

   - If you need to set a **custom** size, enter values into the height and width drop-down menus, choosing inches or centimetres as measurement units in advance—note that the print size changes to "Custom" after entering new values. The Print Size resolution alters automatically while honouring your print Width and Height.

3. Drag out your crop area to create your constrained rectangle or square (if Custom).

4. Double-click the crop area to crop to the designated size.

Use the **Thirds grid** check box on the Context toolbar for improving photo composition. A 3 x 3 rectangular grid with equally spaced lines (two vertically, two horizontally) is superimposed on top of your photo when the check box is selected.

Moving and resizing the grid allows the main subject of your photo (in this case a big wheel) to be offset and balanced against a foreground or background feature within the photo (e.g., the sky as background). Position a main item of interest in the photo where any two lines intersect within the crop grid (four intersections are possible). This is known as the "rule of thirds" which will help you find the most balanced composition where your eyes are drawn to the main subject. Double-click to crop the photo to the outer grid dimensions.

You can also crop an image to any selection region, no matter what shape, as defined with one of the selection tools. For example, here's cropping applied to a selection created with the Magnetic Selection Tool:

Before

After
(Crop to Selection)

To crop the image to the selection:

- Choose **Crop to Selection** from the **Image** menu.

If the selection region is non-rectangular, the left-over surrounding region will be either transparent (on a standard layer) or the current background colour (e.g., white).

 Cropping to the selection affects all image layers. Everything outside the selected region is eliminated.

Flipping and rotating

Flipping and rotating are standard manipulations that you can carry out on the whole image, the active layer, a path, or just on a selection. Flips are used to change the direction of a subject's gaze, fix composition, and so on, whereas rotation is an orientation tool for general purpose use.

Flip Horizontal

Flip Vertical

Rotate
15° anti-clockwise

Rotate
10° clockwise

To flip:

- Choose either **Flip Horizontally** or **Flip Vertically** from the **Image** menu, then select **Image**, **Layer**, **Selection** or **Path** from the submenu.

To rotate:

1. Choose **Rotate** from the **Image** menu.

2. From the flyout menu, select an option based on the object (Image, Layer, or Selection), rotation angle (90° or 180°), and the direction (Clockwise or Anti-clockwise) required.

3. You can also select **Custom...**, to display a Rotate dialog, from which you can do all of the above but instead set your own custom angle, even down to fractional degrees.

Straightening a photo

As an image adjustment, the **Straighten Tool** can be used to align a crooked image back to horizontal (e.g., restoring proper horizontal alignment in a scanned image that wasn't aligned correctly on the scanner). Use the tool to trace a new horizon line against a line in the image—the image automatically orients itself to the drawn horizon line.

Before
(horizon line drawn by
dragging)

After

To straighten:

1. Choose the [icon] **Straighten Tool** from the Crop Tools flyout on the **Tools** toolbar.

2. On the Context toolbar, choose an option from the **Canvas** drop-down list. This lets you decide how your straightened image will be displayed:

*   **Crop** - Crops and adjusts the straightened image so that it displays on the largest possible canvas size, without displaying any border.

*   **Expand to Fit** - Increases the canvas size to display the entire straightened image. The border area is filled with the current background colour.

*   **Original Size** - Displays the straightened image within the original canvas dimensions. The border area is filled with the current background colour.

> On the image that needs straightening, look for a straight line on the image to which you can set the new horizon (e.g., the divide between the mountain and sand above).

3. Using the Straighten cursor, drag a horizon line from one end of the image's line to the other (the length of the horizon line is not important) then release. The image orients itself to the new line.

Deforming

The  **Deform Tool** is a "Jack of all trades" that lets you move, scale, rotate, or skew a selection or layer. Start by making a selection if desired, then choose the Deform Tool. A rectangle appears with handles at its corners and edges, and a fixed point (initially in the centre of the region). If there's no selection, the rectangle includes the whole active layer.

The image opposite has been skewed from a rectangular selection.

The tool's action depends on the exact position of the mouse pointer. As you move the pointer around the enclosed region, the cursor changes as shown below to indicate which action is possible.

To **move the region** without any deformation, drag from its neutral midsection. This action works just like the Move Tool.

To **reshape the region**, drag from an edge or corner handle. A variety of options are available (watch the Hintline for tips).

Over a corner handle:
- Drag to scale region in two dimensions (height and width).
- To maintain constant proportions, drag with the **Shift** key down.
- To scale the region relative to the fixed point, drag with the **Alt** key down. Pixels further from the fixed point will move further than those close to it.
- To freely distort the region from one corner, drag with the **Ctrl** key down.
- To scale relative to the fixed point with constant proportions, drag while pressing **Shift+Alt**.
- To distort relative to the fixed point, drag while pressing **Ctrl+Alt**. The opposite corner mirrors the dragged corner's movement.
- To distort the region along either adjacent edge, drag while pressing **Shift+Ctrl**.
- For a perspective effect, drag while pressing **Shift+Ctrl+Alt**. The adjacent corner mirrors the dragged corner's movement.

Over an edge handle:
- Drag to move the edge in or out, for a squash/stretch effect.
- For a squash/stretch effect relative to the fixed point, drag with the **Alt** key down. Pixels further from the fixed point will move further than those close to it.
- To move the edge freely, for a skew effect, drag with the **Ctrl** key down.
- For a skew effect relative to the fixed point, drag while pressing **Ctrl+Alt**. The opposite edge mirrors the dragged edge's movement.
- For a constrained skew effect, press **Shift+Ctrl** and drag the edge along its line.
- For constrained skew relative to the fixed point, press **Shift+Ctrl+Alt** and drag the edge along its line.

To **rotate the region** about the fixed point, drag from just outside a corner. To constrain rotation in 15-degree steps, press the **Shift** key after you've begun rotation, and hold it down until after you release the mouse button. You can change the location of the fixed point (see below).

To **reposition the fixed point**, move the cursor to the exact centre until a small target appears, then drag. The fixed point can be moved anywhere—even outside the deformation region. Great for arced rotations.

Mesh warping

The 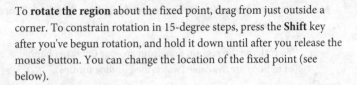 **Mesh Warp Tool** works like the Deform Tool outfitted with complex curves. It lets you define a flexible grid of points and lines that you can drag to distort an image, or part of an image (or layer). You can edit the mesh to vary its curvature, and even custom-design a mesh to match a particular image's geometry—for example, curves that follow facial contours—for more precise control of the warp effect.

> The Mesh Warp Tool works on Background and standard layers, but not on text layers or shape layers.

When you first select the tool, a simple rectangular mesh appears over the image, with nine nodes: one at each corner, one at the centre, and one at the midpoint of each edge. Straight lines connect adjacent nodes. A context toolbar also appears to support the Mesh Warp Tool.

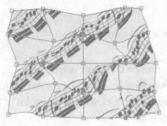

The straight line segments are actually bendable curves. When you alter the contours of the mesh and distort the initial rectangular grid, the underlying image deforms accordingly. To change the mesh, you simply move nodes, node attractor handles, or connecting lines; add or subtract nodes as needed; and/or edit nodes to change the curvature of adjoining lines.

To select a mesh node:

- Click it. (**Shift**-click or drag a marquee to select multiple nodes.)

One or more attractor handles appear on the selected node(s) and on any adjacent nodes. The number of handles per node will vary depending on the number of adjacent nodes.

To warp the mesh:

- Drag a mesh node to move it.
  OR

- Drag a line segment to reshape it.
  OR

- Drag a node's attractor handles.

Unless you're working in Setup mode, the image responds immediately as the mesh is warped. The bendability of line segments depends on the type of nodes at either end. (Both Setup mode and node types are detailed below.)

The **Deform Mesh** option makes it easy to move, scale, skew, or rotate a portion of the mesh about a fixed point. It works just like the standard Deform tool (described above) on multiple nodes.

To deform the mesh systematically:

1. **Shift**-click or drag a marquee to select multiple nodes.

2. Click the [icon] **Deform Mesh** button on the Mesh Warp Tool's Context toolbar. A selection rectangle appears around the designated nodes (you may need to zoom out to see this), with a fixed point in the centre and handles at its corners, sides, and centre.

3. Click to use the **Deform Mesh Tool** to move, scale, or rotate a portion of the region (as defined by nodes) about a fixed point.

   - To deform the mesh region, drag from any corner or midpoint handle.

   - To rotate the mesh region, drag from just outside any corner handle.

   - To move the fixed point, move the cursor over the fixed point symbol until the cursor changes, then drag (this then lets you perform arc rotations). To move the entire region, drag from elsewhere within the region.

   - Watch the HintLine for details on many key-assisted options such as skew, squash/stretch, and perspective effects. In this respect, the tool works almost exactly like the regular Deform Tool (see p. 54).

4. Click the button again to return to standard mode.

To add a new node:

- Double-click on a line segment.
  OR

- Click on a line segment then select the [icon] **Add Node** button on the displayed Context toolbar.

The new node appears, along with extra nodes where the new connecting lines intersect existing lines. Adding a new node further subdivides the mesh.

To delete one or more nodes:

1. Select the node(s).

2. Press **Delete**.
   OR

   Click the **Delete node(s)** button on the displayed Context toolbar.

Deleting a node also deletes lines and nodes connected to it. If you delete a corner or edge node, the overall mesh area will decrease. To delete a specific grid line and its nodes, click to place a marker on the line, then press **Delete**.

The bendability of line segments depends on the type of nodes at either end. You can change a node from one type to another simply by selecting it and using the Context toolbar buttons:

Mesh nodes can be **sharp**, **smooth**, or **symmetric** (see illustrations below). Changing a node's type lets you control how much the curved segments bend on either side of the node. To determine a node's current type, select it and check to see which Mesh Node button on the toolbar is also selected.

To change a node to a different type:

- Select it and click one of the other node buttons.

Experiment, and you'll begin to appreciate the fine control that these settings afford. For example, using a light-blue Quick Grill shape, it's easy to appreciate the difference between node types.

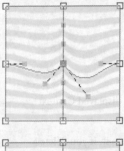

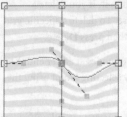

Sharp means that the slope and depth of the curves on either side of the node are completely independent of each other. The contours can be adjusted separately, and the intersection can be pointed.

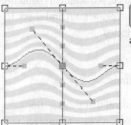

Smooth means that the slope of the curve is the same on both sides of the node, but the depth of the contours on either side can differ.

Symmetric nodes join curves with the same slope and depth on both sides of the node.

To reset the mesh to full-frame and rectangular:

- Click the ⊞ **Reset Mesh** button on the Mesh Context toolbar.

To hide the mesh for a better preview of the image:

- Click the 🄴 **Hide/Show Mesh** button on the Mesh Context toolbar. Click again to reveal the mesh for editing.

Extracting part of an image

The [Extract] button on the Photo Studio toolbar makes light work of isolating a subject from its background (or vice versa).

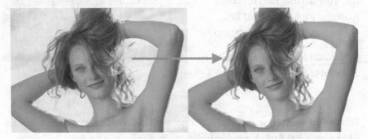

You simply brush an outline around the edges of a region you want to extract from the rest of the image, then mark a "foreground" area to be retained—usually inside the outline. PhotoPlus applies sophisticated edge detection within the marked edge band, decides which pixels to keep, and turns the rest transparent, with variable blending along the edge. In preview mode, you can fine-tune and reapply the extraction settings, and manually touch up the image until the result is just right.

Instead of marking a foreground region, you can designate a specific "key" colour to which edge pixels can be compared. Similar pixels will be kept, and dissimilar pixels discarded. (See PhotoPlus help for details).

Using channels

Every colour photo that you use in PhotoPlus will have channels associated with it. For the colour mode RGB, the individual channels Red (R), Green (G) and Blue (B) make up a composite RGB channel. Alternatively, channels can also be separate, i.e. as their individual colours—Red, Green and Blue. Each channel stores that particular colour's information which, when combined with the other channels, brings about the full colour image.

> Within PhotoPlus, channels are treated as a colour sub-set of the active selected layer, whether this is a background, standard, shape or text layer.

PhotoPlus lets you show, hide, and select composite or specific channels of any photo from a single point, called the Channels tab. This tab lists the composite RGB and each individual Red, Green and Blue channel in turn.

By default, all channels are selected and visible (see opposite).

Why do we want to select channels anyway? This is because you can apply an edit to an individual channel in isolation. Typically, you could:

- Apply a filter effect

- Make an image adjustment

- Paint onto a channel

- Paste selections

- Apply a colour fill

To hide/show channels:

1. Select the **Channels** tab.

2. Decide which channel you want to hide in isolation.

3. Click the eye icon next to the channel (it doesn't have to be selected) to make it hidden. When the icon is clicked again, the channel is made visible.

> ★ To view selected channels in colour rather than greyscale, check the Show Channels in Colour option (click the ▷ button on the tab).

> ★ The composite RGB channel is shown only when all the other channels are shown. When only a single or pair of single channels is shown the composite channel will never be shown.

To select specific channels for edit:

1. Select the **Channels** tab. All channels are switched on and are shown by default.

2. Click on the channel you want to select—the other channels will be deselected and hidden automatically. Use **Shift**-click to include additional channels if necessary.

3. Apply the adjustment, special effect, painting operation, etc. to the selected channel(s).

 When you switch on a channel it is made visible in isolation by default.

Interpreting histograms

The Histogram tab is used to view the distribution of colours and tones spread throughout your current selection, selected layer or entire photo (by default). This gives an opportunity to view and interpret a complete snapshot of the range of colours and, most importantly, the distribution of pixels that adopt those colours.

The histogram doesn't carry out any adjustments by itself, but it is useful for evaluating the kinds of image adjustments that may be needed. This decision is up to the photographer and his/her own personal judgement.

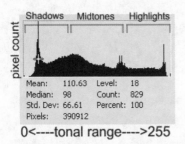

For any channel, the horizontal X axis represents the range of tones, each tone is at a specific level. Think of the histogram as being split into three portions— **Shadows**, **Midtones**, and **Highlights**.

The vertical Y axis is the relative **pixel count** at each of the levels on the X axis described above. The higher the graph is at any level, the more pixels reside at that particular level. Remember that this histogram could refer to a Red, Green, Blue, RGB or luminance channel.

A crosshair cursor lets you move around the histogram, displaying the pixel count for the colour level that your cursor is currently placed at. For example, the tab above shows the cursor at colour level 18 (see the first peak), which has a count of 829 pixels.

You can choose to view the histogram for an individual Red, Green or Blue channel, or the composite of the three, the RGB channel. Luminance (or lightness) can also be shown.

To view a specific channel:

- Click the ▷ **Tab Menu** button at the top right of the tab to reveal a flyout. To change to a different channel, pick a channel from the list or display statistics (as shown above) by checking **Show Statistics**.

4

Painting and Drawing

Choosing colours

Foreground and background colours

At any given time, PhotoPlus allows you to work with just two colours—a **foreground** colour and a **background** colour. These are always visible as two swatches on the Colour tab indicated opposite (ringed).

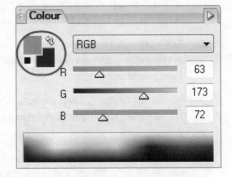

The foreground colour is set to green (RGB 63:173:73) and the background colour to black.

Now, a few things to remember about how these colours are used:

- When you paint with one of the brush tools, add text, or draw a line or shape, left-dragging (that is, dragging with the left mouse button down) applies the foreground colour. For example, for a company logo:

  The additional darker areas of the photo can be added after swapping foreground and background colours over using the tab's ⤸ button.

- When you cut, delete, or erase an area on the Background layer, the area exposes the background colour—as if that colour were there "behind" the portion of the image being removed. (By the way, layers other than the Background behave differently: on these, a removed area exposes transparency.)

Electronic artists expend much of their creative energy deciding which of the millions of available colours should fill those two slots. The actual steps involved, however, can be quite simple.

To define foreground and background colour:

1. Select the  **Colour Pickup Tool** on the **Tools** toolbar.

2. Left-click with the tool anywhere on an image to "pick up" the colour at that point as the new foreground colour. Right-click to define a new background colour.

3. (Optional) On the Context toolbar, set the **Sample Size** (pickup region) as a single "Point Sample" or a "3 x 3 Average" or "5 x 5 Average" area.

> To switch temporarily to the Colour Pickup Tool from a paint, line, shape, fill, or text tool, hold down the Alt key, then click to define the foreground colour.

OR

1. On the Colour tab, move the mouse pointer (dropper cursor) around the **Colour Spectrum**. As you move the dropper cursor around the spectrum, the preview swatch to the upper left of the spectrum shows the colour at the cursor position.

2. Left-click in the spectrum to set a new foreground colour, and right-click to set a new background colour.

> You can change this RGB spectrum to display in Greyscale, or show the colours spread between the Foreground/Background colours (click the ▷ button on the tab).

OR

1. On the Colour tab, click either the foreground or the background swatch.

2. Use the slider(s) or enter numeric values in the boxes to define a specific colour. The selected swatch updates instantly.

> ✦ To swap foreground and background colours, click the ⇄ double arrow button next to the swatches. To reset the colours to black and white, click the black and white mini-swatch at the bottom left of the swatch.
>
> ✦ Clicking an active swatch will also let you apply a chosen colour from the Adjust Colour dialog's colour wheel, and will let you define and store that colour in a set of custom colours.

The Colour tab makes it possible to set the working colour model: **RGB** (Red, Green, Blue); **CMYK** (Cyan, Magenta, Yellow, Black); **HSL** sliders (Hue, Saturation, Lightness); **HSL Colour Wheel**; **HSL Colour Box**; or **Greyscale**. models

To set the mode:

- Choose an option from the 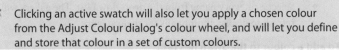 drop-down list.

Storing colours

If you want to save colours that you want to work with frequently, you can store them in the Swatches tab as thumbnails (this avoids continually defining colours in the Colour tab). The **Swatches tab** hosts galleries of categorized colour thumbnails.

You can store your own frequently used colours to the Default category (or any currently selected category, e.g. Colour_Gall_53) by using the Colour tab or Colour Pickup Tool; you can also create categories yourself into which you can add your own thumbnails.

The Swatches tab also lets you choose pre-defined colours from a range of "themed" categories (e.g., Earth, Fruits, Pastel, and Web browser safe).

To add, edit or delete a Gallery category:

- Click **Add Category...** from the Swatches tab's ▷ **Tab Menu** button and enter a name in the dialog. You can also **Edit Category...** or **Delete Category** from the same location.

To choose a Gallery category:

- Select a category name from the drop-down list. The gallery will refresh to display thumbnails for that category.

To add a colour to the Swatches tab:

1. Either:

    Choose a colour from the Colour tab's colour spectrum.
    OR
    Select the **Colour Pickup Tool** and hover over then click on a chosen colour.

    You'll notice the Colour tab's foreground colour swatch change.

2. From the Swatches tab, pick the correct category to store the colour.

3. Click the ⊞ **New Swatch** button to add the foreground colour to the current gallery.

To apply a colour from the Swatches tab:

- Select any gallery thumbnail then paint, draw, fill, etc. Note that a thumbnail click will change the Colour tab's foreground colour.

Painting

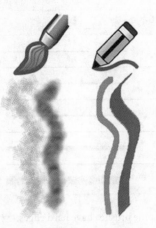

The ✏ **Paintbrush Tool** and ✎ **Pencil Tool** on the **Tools** toolbar are the basic tools for painting and drawing freehand lines on the active layer. They work on Background and standard layers, but not on text layers or shape layers. The tools work by changing pixels on the layer's bitmap plane.

💡 Successful freehand drawing requires practice and a steady hand! You might find it easier if you use a graphics tablet if available, rather than a mouse.

The Paintbrush Tool will always apply **antialiasing** to its brush strokes without exception. For the most part this is ideal as brush edges will appear very smooth—irrespective of the Hardness setting of your current brush. However, how can a hard-edged brush effect be achieved? This is possible with the **Pencil Tool**, a hard-edged brush tool which is used just like the Paintbrush Tool but always with the hard-edging.

The **Brush Tip tab** hosts a comprehensive collection of brush presets grouped into various categories; each category can be switched to via a drop-down list (the "Basic" category is shown opposite) and displays a gallery. Note that each sample clearly shows the brush tip and stroke; the number indicates the brush diameter. The brush tip determines the thickness and many other properties of the painted line.

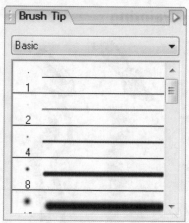

If you scroll down the gallery, you'll note that some brushes have hard edges, while others appear fuzzy, with soft edges. The hardness of a brush is expressed as a percentage of its full diameter. If less than 100%, the brush has a soft edge region within which the opacity of applied colour falls off gradually.

Brush attributes (blend mode, opacity, size, and flow) can be modified via a context toolbar (along with more advanced Brush Options) and, if necessary, saved for future use with the Tool Presets tab.

If a more bespoke brush tip is required, you can also customize your own brush tip and save it in its own user-defined category. (See PhotoPlus help for details.)

An important factor when applying brush strokes is the level of opacity applied to the brush. This attribute affects brush strokes significantly when the stroke is applied onto already transparent standard layers. The greater the opacity the more opaque the brush stroke, and vice versa. Experiment to achieve the right combination of opacity and colour for your brush strokes.

To use the Paintbrush or Pencil tool:

1. Select the ![paintbrush icon] **Paintbrush Tool** or ![pencil icon] **Pencil Tool** from the **Tools** toolbar's Brush flyout. When you move the tool over the image the cursor will change.

2. Choose a brush tip preset on the Brush Tip tab. If you've picked a Basic brush, set a brush colour (i.e. the foreground colour) from the Colour tab before painting. You can also create your own brush from within the tab.

3. Change brush tip's attributes, if necessary, on the Context toolbar. These changes do not affect the brush presets present in the Brush Tip tab. Click the **Brush** option to reveal the Brush Options dialog, which lets you set more advanced brush characteristics.

4. Drag the cursor on the active layer, holding the left mouse button down to paint in the foreground colour.

Stamping and spraying pictures

The ![picture brush icon] **Picture Brush Tool** works like a custom brush that sprays a series of pre-defined or custom images at regular intervals as you drag. Used in conjunction with the Brush Tip tab you can select from a variety of picture brushes in different categories, and you can import Paint Shop Pro "picture tubes."

You can use the tool either to "stamp" single images at specific points or lay out a continuous stream of repeating pictures as in the letter "S" on the left.

The Picture Brush tool works on Background and standard layers, but not on text layers or shape layers.

To draw with the Picture Brush:

1. Choose the **Picture Brush Tool** and (on the Brush Tip tab) pick a brush tip from one of the categories.

2. To "stamp" single images at specific points, click in various places on your canvas. To spray a continuous line of images, drag a path across the page.

You can scale the size of the image elements produced by the tool, and control the spacing and sequencing of elements for individual brush tips via the Context toolbar, set the image **Diameter** to be higher or lower as needed.

Note that this isn't an absolute setting, but a relative one. Each picture brush stores its own pre-defined elements, and this scaling determines how the tool scales elements up or down when drawing. The actual size of stored elements varies between brushes, so you may need to adjust the image diameter when switching between different brushes.

To control image elements, right-click a brush sample from any Brush Tip tab category, and choose **Brush Options...**. Adjust **Spacing** to determine how closely elements are packed together, or set the **Order** to present elements Randomly, Sequentially (as per the preset thumbnail) or By direction (according to stroke).

To import a Paint Shop Pro picture tube file:

1. On the Brush Tip tab, right-click any brush tip from any category and choose **Import...**.

2. Use the dialog to browse for and select the picture tube (.TUB) file to import.

If you right-click on any gallery sample, you can manage categories, and access brush options. With a bit of forethought, it's not difficult to lay out your own master images and from them create your own custom Picture Brush tips. (For details, see online help.)

Erasing

Sometimes the rubber end of the pencil can be just as important to an artist as the pointed one. The Eraser Tools flyout on the **Tools** toolbar provides ways of enhancing an image by "painting" with transparency rather than with colour:

The **Standard Eraser Tool** for replacing colours in an image either with the background colour or with transparency (on Background or other standard layers, respectively).

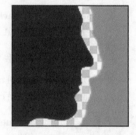

The **Background Eraser Tool** for erasing pixels similar to a sampled reference colour underlying the cursor crosshair—great for painting out unwanted background colours, e.g. when isolating objects or people photographed against a studio backdrop.

The **Flood Eraser Tool** for filling a region with transparency, erasing pixels similar to the colour under the cursor when you first click.

In general, you can set tool properties for each tool including brush characteristics, opacity, tolerance, flow, and choose a brush tip. The Eraser tools work on Background and standard layers, but not on text layers or shape layers.

To erase with the Standard Eraser:

1. Select the **Standard Eraser Tool** from the **Tools** toolbar's Eraser Tools flyout.

2. (Optional) Change properties, especially brush **Size** and **Opacity**, on the Context toolbar.
   For erasing with an airbrush effect or hard-edged brush, check the **Airbrush** or **Hard Edge** option.

3. Drag with the tool on the active layer. On the Background layer, erased pixels expose the current background colour. On other layers, they expose transparency.

To erase with the Background Eraser:

1. Select the **Background Eraser Tool** from the **Tools** toolbar's Eraser Tools flyout.

2. (Optional) Change properties on the Context toolbar.

3. Drag with the tool on the active layer to erase pixels similar to a sampled reference colour.

   - With "Contiguous" limits (default), the tool erases only within-tolerance pixels adjacent to each other and within the brush width; this tends to restrict erasure to one side of an edge or line. When you set "Discontiguous" limits, all matching pixels are erased under the brush even if they are non-adjacent (great for removing uniform background like sky). The "Edge Detected" setting can improve erasure along one side of a contrasting edge or line.

Contiguous   Discontiguous

- With "Continual" sampling (the default), the reference colour is repeatedly updated as you move the cursor. Sampling "Once" means erasure is based on the colour under the crosshair when you first click. Use the "Background Swatch" setting to use the current background colour (Colour tab) as the reference.

- You also have the option of protecting the current foreground colour from erasure (**Protect foreground**).

> 🖎 If you use the tool on the Background layer, it's promoted to a standard layer.

To erase with the Flood Eraser:

1. Select the 🖎 **Flood Eraser Tool** from the **Tools** toolbar's Eraser Tools flyout.

2. (Optional) Change properties on the Context toolbar.

3. Drag with the tool on the active layer to erase pixels close in colour (based on the Tolerance range) to the colour under the cursor when you first click. If you use the tool on the Background layer, it's promoted to a standard layer.

   - The **Tolerance** setting determines the breadth of the colour range to be erased.

   - The **Opacity** setting will alter the erased areas level of transparency.

   - Check **Contiguous** to erase only within-tolerance pixels connected to each other; when unchecked, all in-range pixels are erased.

   - Check **Use All Layers** to take colour boundaries on other layers into account, although erasure happens only on the current layer.

   - **Antialias** smooths the boundary between the erased area and the remaining area.

Using patterns

The  **Pattern Tool** lets you paint a pattern directly onto your canvas. In effect, it "clones" any pattern bitmap you've selected while providing the flexibility to paint wherever you wish, and control opacity, blend mode, and so on. Like the Clone Tool, the Pattern brush picks up pixels from a source—in this case, the bitmap pattern—and deposits them where you're drawing. You can choose a pre-defined, tiled bitmap pattern from the Patterns dialog, or define your own patterns.

As an example, patterns can be used effectively as a painted background when creating web graphics.

To paint with a pattern:

1. Select the **Pattern Tool** from the **Tools** toolbar's Clone flyout.

2. On the Context toolbar, choose your brush attributes (see p. 65) and click the **Pattern** thumbnail to display the Patterns dialog. To select from various pattern categories, right-click any of the thumbnails and choose a different category from the bottom of the flyout menu. Simply click a pattern to select it. Other right-click options let you edit the pattern categories or add new patterns from stored bitmap files.

3. To paint, drag with the tool on the active layer (or in the current selection).

★ The Aligned check box in the Context toolbar determines what happens each time you begin brushing in a new place. If checked, the pattern extends itself seamlessly with each new brush stroke; if unchecked, it begins again each time you click the mouse.

Creating your own patterns

The built-in selection of patterns in the Patterns dialog provides a useful starting point, but you can also create your own patterns from any selection, or even the whole image. And take a look at the Tile Maker effect if you have a relatively small sample region (like a patch of grass) and want to produce a pattern from it that can be tiled seamlessly over a broader area.

To create a new pattern:

1. Define a selection if you wish, and choose **Create Pattern...** from the **Edit** menu.

2. To store the pattern, select a user-defined category from the dialog's **Category** drop-down menu (or keep with the default My Patterns category).

3. Click **OK**.

A thumbnail appears in the category gallery, ready to brush on (or use as a brush tip texture or fill) at any time. Right-clicking any pattern lets you rename the pattern categories or add new patterns from stored bitmap files.

Filling a region

Filling regions or layers is an alternative to brushing on colours or patterns. Making a selection prior to applying a fill, and setting appropriate options, can spell the difference between a humdrum effect and a spectacular one.

The **Fill Tools flyout** on the **Tools** toolbar includes two tools for filling regions with colour and/or transparency: **Flood Fill** and **Gradient Fill**. In addition, you can use the **Edit>Fill...** command to apply either a **colour** or **pattern** fill. As with paint tools, if there is a selection, the Fill tools only affect pixels within the selected region. If you're operating on a shape or text layer, a single fill affects the interior of the object(s) on the layer.

Flood and pattern fills

The ◆ **Flood Fill Tool** works on Background and standard layers, replacing an existing colour region with the foreground colour. How large a region is "flooded" with the fill colour depends on the difference between the colour of the pixel you initially click and the colour of surrounding pixels.

You can use the Context toolbar to set a **tolerance** value—how much of a colour difference the tool looks for. With a low tolerance setting, the tool "gives up easily" and only fills pixels very close in colour to the one you click (a setting of 0 would fill only pixels of the same colour; 255 would fill all pixels). As the tolerance increases, so does the tool's effect on pixels further in colour from the original pixel, so a larger region is flooded.

When **Antialias** is checked, the boundary of a colour fill is smoothed; uncheck to produce a hard edge to the fill boundary.

When checked, **Contiguous** affects only pixels connected to the clicked pixel; uncheck to affect in-range pixels throughout the region.

The Context toolbar includes an **All Layers** option. If checked, the Flood Fill tool samples pixels on all layers (both shown and hidden) underlying the click point, as if the layers were merged into one. If unchecked, it only samples pixels on the active layer. In either case, it only fills pixels on the active layer.

A pattern can be applied as a fill from the Context toolbar by picking a **Pattern** (click the thumbnail) from the gallery, then choosing the **Fill** drop down list to be "Pattern".

To use the Flood Fill Tool:

1. Select the ◆ **Flood Fill Tool** from the **Tools** toolbar's Fill Tools flyout.

2. Set tolerance and layer fill options (see above) on the Context toolbar.

3. Click with the tool where you want to start the fill.

The **Edit>Fill...** command lets you flood-fill a region on a standard layer using any colour, not just the foreground colour. On the other hand, it's strictly a solid colour flood without the subtleties of the Flood Fill Tool's properties. Simply choose the command to display the Fill dialog.

Fill

Type: Colour ▼   OK

● Foreground   Cancel
○ Background
○ Custom: [   ]

Blend Options

Mode: Normal ▼

Opacity: 100 ÷ %

☐ Preserve Transparency

To use the Fill command:

- Choose **Fill...** from the **Edit** menu. The Fill dialog appears.

- For a flood fill, set the **Type** to **Colour.**

- Choose whether the fill colour is to be the current **Foreground** colour, **Background** colour or a **Custom** colour.

- Specify the blend mode and opacity of the fill.
  If you check **Preserve Transparency**, transparent areas will resist the flood colour; otherwise, everything in the selection or layer will be equally washed with the fill.

- For a Pattern fill, set the **Type** to **Pattern**.
  The blend options are the same, but in this mode instead of choosing a colour you can fill a region with any pattern stored in the Patterns dialog. Click the pattern sample to bring up the gallery of pattern thumbnails, then right-click any thumbnail to choose a category from the bottom of the list. (See Using patterns on p. 78.)

Gradient Fill Tool

Whereas solid fills use a single colour, all gradient fills in PhotoPlus utilize at least two "key" colours, with a spread of hues in between each key colour, creating a "spectrum" effect. You can fine-tune the actual spread of colour between pairs of key colours. Likewise, a gradient fill in PhotoPlus can have either **solid transparency**—one level of opacity, like 50% or 100%, across its entire range—or **variable transparency**, with at least two "key" opacity levels and a spread of values in between. (Remember that opacity is simply an inverse way of expressing transparency.)

The [icon] **Gradient Fill Tool** lets you apply variable colour and/or transparency fills directly to a layer. Five types of fill (Solid, Linear, Radial, Conical, and Square) are available. Technically, a Solid fill is different (it uses just one colour) but in practice you can also achieve a unicolour effect using a gradient fill.

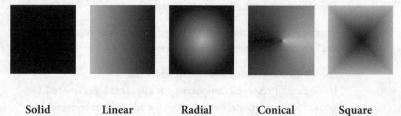

| Solid | Linear | Radial | Conical | Square |

Applying a gradient fill on any kind of layer entails selecting one of the fill types, editing the fill colours and/or transparency in a Gradient dialog, then applying the fill. However, gradient fills behave differently depending on the kind of layer you're working on.

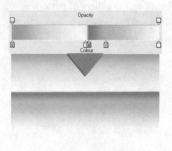

On **standard and Background layers**, the tool creates a "spectrum" effect, filling the active layer or selection with colours spreading between the key colours in the selected gradient fill. The fill is applied rather like a coat of spray paint over existing pixels on the layer; colour and transparency properties in the fill gradient interact with the existing pixels to produce new values.

Transparency works in a comparable way, affecting how much the paint you apply is "thinned." At full opacity, the fill completely obscures pixels underneath.

On **text and shape layers**, the Gradient Fill Tool is even more powerful—the fill's colour and transparency properties remain editable. Technically, the fill is a property of the layer, and the shape(s) act as a "window" enabling you to see the fill. Thus a single fill applies to all the shapes on a particular layer—note the gradient fill opposite which is applied across three QuickShapes present on the same layer.

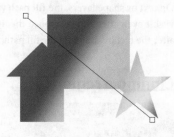

Transparency gradients determines which portions of the object you can see through. Note that the Flood Fill Tool doesn't work with text or shapes. When first drawn, a shape takes a Solid fill using the foreground colour. You can change the fill type as described below.

To apply a gradient fill:

1. Select **Gradient Fill Tool** from the **Tools** toolbar's Fill flyout.

2. Select a fill type from the Context toolbar. Choose Linear, Radial, Conical or Square.

3. To choose a preset or to edit the fill's colours and/or transparency values, click the colour sample on the Context toolbar. The Gradient dialog appears, which either offers a range of selectable presets in the upper gallery (right-click to pick a different themed gallery from the drop-down list) or a lower fill spectrum for creating custom fills (from a preset or from scratch). See PhotoPlus help for details on how to edit gradient fills.

4. Once you've defined the fill, click with the tool where you want to start the fill and drag to the point where you want it to end.

To change a text or shape layer's fill type, or edit its colour(s):

*   Double-click the shape layer (or right-click and choose **Edit Fill...**).
    OR
    Choose the **Gradient Fill Tool** and use the Context toolbar.

Either option lets you choose a fill type, and/or click the colour (or gradient) sample to edit the fill.

On text or shape layers, the **fill path** (the line in the illustration above) remains visible even after you've applied the fill, and you can adjust the fill's placement after the fact by dragging the fill path's end nodes with the Gradient Fill Tool.

Cloning a region

The  **Clone Tool** is like two magic brushes locked together. While you trace or "pick up" an original drawing with one brush, the other draws ("puts down") an exact duplicate somewhere else—even in another image.

When retouching, for example, you can remove an unwanted object from an image by extending another area of the image over it (note the pickup area is positioned over the sea rather than the original boat).

The tool acts on the active Background or standard layer, and can even clone **all** layers (including Text layers or Shape layers).

To clone a region:

1. Select the **Clone Tool** on the **Tools** toolbar's Clone flyout.

2. Change properties, if necessary, on the Context toolbar. For example:

   - Reducing the tool's **Opacity** setting results in a "ghosted" copy of the original pixels.

   - For additional brush strokes, to always reuse the original pickup point, keep **Aligned** unchecked. Check **Aligned** to have your pickup point change to be offset in relation to your brush tip's position—great for removing unwanted regions that follow a natural path (e.g., a tree branch).

Aligned unchecked   Aligned checked

   - (Optional) For multiple layers, the context toolbar hosts a **Use all layers** option which, when checked, will clone **all** layers (including Background, standard, Text and Shape layers together). When unchecked, only the active (selected) layer is cloned.

3. To define the pickup origin, **Shift**-click with the tool.

4. Click again where you want to start the copy, then drag to paint the copy onto the new location. Repeat as needed. A crosshair marks the pickup point, which moves relative to your brush movements.

Creating and editing text

PhotoPlus makes use of two text tools, i.e.

- The **[A]** **Text Tool**, for entering solid, colourful text on a new layer.

- The **[A]** **Text Selection Tool**, for creating a selection in the shape of text (for filling with unusual fills).

The Layers tab designates **text layers** with a **T** symbol. Like shapes, solid text in PhotoPlus is **editable**: as long as it remains on a separate text layer, you can retype it or change its properties at a later date.

To create new solid text:

1. Click **[A▼]** **Text Tools** (**Tools** toolbar), then the **[A]** **Text Tool**.

2. Click on your image with the text cursor to set where you want to insert text. The text attributes (font, point size, bold/italic/underline, alignment, antialias and colour) set on the Text Context toolbar prior to clicking will be applied.
   OR

   Drag across the page to size your text according to requirements. Release the mouse button to set the point size.

3. Type your text, which is applied directly on your page. The text appears on a new transparent layer in the image. You can now use the Move Tool or other tools and commands to manipulate it, just like the contents of any layer.

To edit text:

1. Select all or part of any text.

2. On the Text Context toolbar, set new text attributes (font, point size, bold/italic/underline, alignment, antialias, or colour) to be adopted by the selected text area. The **Character** tab also lets you adjust selected text's Point Size, letter Spacing, Leading, Advance, or Width.

To change text's solid colour:

1. Select all or part of any text.

2. Click the colour swatch on the Context toolbar and use the Adjust Colour dialog. (See Choosing colours on p. 67) .

3. Select your new colour and click **OK**.

To swap to a gradient colour:

1. On the **Layers** tab, right-click the Text layer and choose **Edit Fill...**.

2. Change the **Fill Type** from **Solid** to one of Linear, Radial, Conical, or Square.

3. Click on the **Fill** gradient swatch and select a preset gradient fill or create your own gradient from the dialog (see Filling a region on p. 79). The gradient fill is immediately applied to your text.

> This applies a gradient fill to all of your text on the layer and not to selected text.

To convert any text layer to a standard layer:

*   Right-click on the layer name and choose **Rasterize** from the menu.

To edit existing text:

1. With the text layer to be edited as the active layer, choose the standard **Text Tool** and move the mouse pointer over the text until it changes to the (I-beam) cursor.

2. Click on or drag to select areas of text—this lets you insert or overwrite selected text, respectively. Equally, you can select areas of text to change font, point size, antialias, and bold/italic/underline attributes—all made from the Text Context toolbar.

> Fine-tune your character size and positioning by using the **Character tab**.

To create a text selection:

1. Click the **Text Tools** flyout (**Tools** toolbar) and choose the ⬛ **Text Selection Tool**.

2. Click at the location on the image where you want to begin the selection.
   OR

   Drag across the page to size your text selection according to requirements. Release the mouse button to set the point size.

3. (Optional) On the Text Context toolbar, set the selection text attributes to be adopted by the new selection (e.g., the font and point size).

4. Type your text directly onto the page.

5. When you're done, click the ✓ **OK** button on the Context toolbar. A selection marquee appears around the text's outline.

6. You can now cut, copy, move, modify, and of course fill the selection.

🔖 Unlike solid text, the text selection doesn't occupy a separate layer.

Drawing and editing lines and shapes

For drawing and editing lines and shapes, the **Tools** toolbar includes the following drawing tool flyouts:

⬛ The **QuickShape Tools** flyout featuring an assortment of tools for creating rectangles, ellipses, polygons, and other shapes.

✏ The **Outline Tools** flyout features various outlines—straight lines, plus freehand and curved outlines for variety.

Overview

Each of the drawing tools has its own creation and editing rules, as detailed below. Before continuing, let's cover some things that all shape objects have in common:

- Shapes have outlines known as **paths**. In a nutshell, shapes as discussed here are **filled** outlines (i.e., they're closed, with colour inside). Later, we'll cover **unfilled** outlines (paths) separately, and consider their special properties. The various drawing tools are all path-drawing tools, applicable to both the filled and unfilled kind of outline.

- Unlike painted regions you create on **raster** (bitmap) layers, both QuickShapes and outline shapes are **vector objects** that occupy special **shape layers**, marked with an symbol on the Layers tab. Each shape layer includes a path thumbnail representing the shape(s) on that layer.

- A QuickShape or straight outline can be drawn directly as a **shape layer**, **path** or as a filled **bitmap**. The Context toolbar hosts buttons which allow you to decide how your lines and shapes are to be drawn, i.e.

   Shape Layer—create your QuickShape or outline on a new shape layer or add to an existing shape layer.

  Paths—add your shape or outline directly as a path rather than as a new/existing shape layer. (See Using paths on p. 98).

  Fill Bitmaps—creates a filled bitmap of the shape or straight outline on a raster layer (e.g., the Background layer).

Curved and freehand outlines cannot be drawn as filled bitmaps.

Assuming you're working on a non-shape layer when you create a shape, the new shape appears on a new shape layer. But what about the next shape you create? Shape layers can store more than one shape, and it's up to you where the next one will go.

This decision is made easy by use of the Context toolbar when the QuickShape or outline tool is selected. The toolbar displays a series of **combination buttons** which determine the layer on which the shape will be placed and the relationship the new shape will have on any existing shapes on the same layer.

 New—Adds the shape to a new shape layer.

Add—Adds the shape to the currently selected layer.

Subtract—removes overlap region when a new shape is added over existing shapes on the currently selected layer. The new shape itself is not included.

Intersect—includes the intersection area only when a new shape is added onto existing selected shapes on the currently selected layer.

Exclude—excludes the intersection area when a new shape is added onto existing selected shapes on the currently selected layer.

To change the fill type, or edit its colour(s):

- Double-click the shape layer.
  OR
  Choose the Gradient Fill Tool and use the Context toolbar.

  Either approach lets you add a spectrum fill, a solid colour fill, and/or a transparency gradient to a shape or text object. For details on changing fills, see the subtopic Gradient Fill Tool.

- A single fill is shared by all the shapes on a particular layer. (Technically the fill is a property of the layer, and the shape(s) act like a "window" that lets you see the fill.) So if you want to draw a red box and a yellow box, for example, you'll need two shape layers.

You can also alter a shape layer's **Opacity** using the Layers tab.

Creating and editing QuickShapes

QuickShapes in PhotoPlus are pre-designed, filled contours that let you instantly add all kinds of shapes to your page, then adjust and vary them using control handles—for innumerable possibilities!

The **QuickShape Tools** flyout lets you choose from a wide variety of commonly used shapes, including boxes, ovals, arrows, polygons, stars, and more. Each shape has its own built-in "intelligent" properties, which you can use to customize the basic shape.

QuickShapes can also be drawn as paths as described elsewhere in Using paths (see p. 98).

To create a QuickShape :

1. Click the ⬜ **QuickShape Tools** flyout on the **Tools** toolbar and select a shape from the flyout menu. (To choose the most recently used shape, just click the toolbar button directly.)

2. Ensure the ⬚ **Shape Layers** button is selected on the Context toolbar.

3. If creating the shape on a new layer, make sure the ⬛ **New** button on the Context toolbar is selected. If creating multiple shapes on the same layer, select one of the other combination buttons on the Context Bar (see above) to specify how the multiple shapes will interact (see above).

4. Select a foreground colour, and any other characteristics for the QuickShape.

5. Drag out the shape on the image. It displays as an outline; hold down the **Ctrl** key while drawing to constrain the aspect ratio. Once drawn, the shape takes a Solid fill using the Colour tab's foreground colour.

To create a filled bitmap from your QuickShape instead, choose the **Fill Bitmaps** button instead of the Shape Layers button.

Each QuickShape is adjustable, so you can experiment before committing to a particular figure and edit it later—with innumerable possibilities!

If you switch to the **Node Edit Tool**, you can adjust the shape. The number of displayed "edit" control handles varies according to the shape; for example, the rectangle has just one control, the polygon has two, and the star has four.

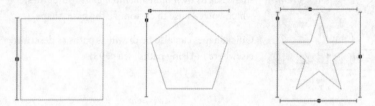

As an example, dragging the side control handle on the middle Quick Pentagon shape downwards will morph the shape to a hexagon, heptagon, octagon, and so on. Dragging the top control handle to the right will rotate the shape in an anti-clockwise direction.

To edit a QuickShape:

1. Click its layer or path name in the Layers or Paths tab, respectively, to select it. If on a Shape layer, make sure the layer's path thumbnail is **selected** to allow the path to be edited with the Node Edit Tool or Shape Edit Tool, i.e.

Path thumbnail   Path thumbnail
selected   deselected

2. Use either:

   - The **Node Edit Tool** (**Tools** toolbar) to click on the shape and readjust any of the shape's handles.
     OR

   - The **Shape Edit Tool** (see below for editing outline shapes) to select, move, resize, and deform individual shapes.

(If you only have one shape on a layer, you can use the **Move Tool** and **Deform Tool**.) To resize without constraint, you can drag any shape's handle; to constrain the shape's proportions, hold down the **Shift** key while dragging. To deform the shape, drag a node while the **Ctrl** key is pressed.

Creating and editing outline shapes

Outline shapes are shapes you draw yourself with Outline tools from the **Tools** toolbar's Outline Tool flyout.

The **Straight Outline Tool** produces an antialiased straight line in PhotoPlus, which is just a very thin shape. The line can be of varying **Weight** (thickness) and can be constrained to 15-degree increments, by holding down the **Shift** key as you drag.

The **Freehand Outline Tool**, as its name implies, lets you draw a squiggly line made up of consecutive line segments and nodes (each new segment starting from another's end node), which can be attached back to itself to create a closed shape. Use the **Smoothness** setting on the Context toolbar to even out ragged contours automatically.

The **Curved Outline Tool** can produce complex combination curves and shapes in a highly controlled way.

Each tool's supporting context toolbar lets you create the outline shape on a shape layer, as a path or directly as a filled bitmap. Additionally, combination buttons let you add the shape to its own layer (or path), and can also be used to control how the new shape interacts with existing shapes on the layer.

Besides being useful with QuickShapes, the Node Edit and Shape Edit tools really come into their own to edit outline shapes.

To edit an outline shape:

1. Click its layer name to select the layer.

2. To move, resize, scale, skew, or rotate the outline, choose the **Shape Edit Tool** . This deform tool works by manipulation of the bounding box around the shape—drag on a corner or edge. (For details on its use, see Deforming on p. 54.)

3. To reshape the outline, choose the **Node Edit Tool**. The outline consists of **line segments** and **nodes** (points where the line segments meet). You can drag one or more individual nodes, or click and drag directly on a line segment.

When you select a node, control handles for the adjacent outline segments appear; each segment in the line has a control handle at either end. The selected node is drawn with a red centre, with the control handle(s) attached to the nodes by blue lines.

Any node can be one of several node types: **sharp**, **smooth**, or **symmetric**. Depending on node type, the node's control handles behave a bit differently, as you can tell with a bit of experimentation. Essentially, the node type determines the slope and curvature of each adjoining segment, and can be chosen from the Context toolbar, i.e.

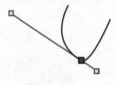 **Sharp Corner** means that the segments either side of the node are completely independent so that the corner can be quite pointed.

 **Smooth Corner** means that the slope of the outline is the same on both sides of the node, but the depth of the two joined segments can be different.

Symmetric Corner nodes join outline segments with the same slope and depth on both sides of the node.

To edit a node:

1. Select it with the Node Edit Tool.

2. Drag its control handle(s) to fine-tune the curve.

You can also use the context toolbar to define a line segment as either straight or curved.

To add a node, double-click on a line segment. To remove a selected node, press the **Delete** key.

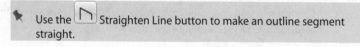

★ Use the Straighten Line button to make an outline segment straight.

Creating outlines

Two approaches to creating outlines are available within PhotoPlus—creating an outline from any current **selection** and creating outlines around layer objects, especially text and shapes (as a **layer effect**). You'll primarily create outlines around text and other objects so the latter method is predominantly used (but we'll cover both!).

Selection
(before and after)

Text
(before and after)

For any outline, you can set the outline width, solid colour, opacity, and choose a blend mode. The outline can also sit inside, outside, or be centred on the selection or object edge.

An outline layer effect can also take a gradient fill, a pattern fill, or a unique **contour** fill (fill runs from the inner to outer edge of the outline width); another advantage over outlines made from selections is the ability to switch the layer object outline off/on, and complement the outline with other layer effects such as Drop Shadow, Glow, Bevel, etc. at the same time.

To create an outline from a selection:

1. Create a selection on a standard or background layer ((but not on Text or Shape layers). (See Making a selection on p. 31).

2. Either:

   - Right-click and select **Outline....**
     OR

   - Pick the same option from the **Edit** menu.

3. From the dialog, choose a **Width** for the outline.

4. Select an outline colour from the drop-down list. The **Foreground** option sets the currently set foreground colour; **Background** sets the current background colour. (See Choosing colours on p. 67). For a **Custom** colour, click the Colour swatch, and select a colour from the displayed Adjust Colour dialog.

5. (Optional) From the **Mode** drop-down menu, pick a blend mode, which controls how the outline colour and underlying pixels blend to make a combined resulting colour. Select the percentage **Opacity** for the outline when blending, and check **Preserve Transparency** to make transparent areas resist the flood colour; otherwise, everything in the selection or layer will be equally washed with the fill.

6. Click **OK**. The outline appears around the selection area.

Once applied, selection outlines no longer remain editable, although if you're not happy with your outline you can still Undo.

To create outlines on a layer (as a layer effect):

1. From the Layers tab, select a layer to which outlines will be applied. Note that all objects (Shapes, Text, or lines) on the layer will be affected.

2. Click the [⚡] **Layer Effects** button on the Layers tab and check **Outline** in the Layer Effects dialog.

3. (Optional) From the **Blend Mode** drop-down menu, pick a blend mode, which controls how the outline colour and underlying pixels blend to make a combined resulting colour. Select the percentage **Opacity** for the outline when blending.

4. Choose a **Width** for the outline, and whether the outline **Alignment** is "Outside" or "Inside" the object's edge (or placed in the "Centre").

5. To set a fill for your outline, pick from the **Fill type** drop-down menu, one of: **Solid**, **Linear**, **Radial**, **Conical**, **Square**, **Contour**, or **Pattern**. Choosing **Solid** will display a colour swatch which, when clicked, shows the Adjust Colour dialog. For other fills, click the gradient fill swatch and apply/edit your gradient fill accordingly (see Editing a gradient fill in PhotoPlus help for details). Pattern fills can be applied via a clickable Pattern swatch (see Using patterns on p. 78 for details).

6. Click **OK**. The outline appears around any layer object.

You may notice the ⚡ icon appear next to the layer with your outline applied.

Remember that you'll be able to apply a combination of 2D layer effects along with your outline, by checking other options in the Layer Effects dialog. See Overview:Applying special effects on p. 113 for more details.

To switch off the layer effect:

- With the layer selected, click the ⚡ **Layer Effects** button and uncheck **Outline** in the Layer Effects dialog.

Using paths

Paths are basically outlines. As such, every filled shape you draw has a path— namely the outline that defines it. In fact, each shape layer has its own path thumbnail next to the layer name, representing the shape(s) that reside on that layer. But more significantly, the concept of a path extends to **independent paths**: unfilled outlines that don't reside on any particular layer, but which are created separately and can be applied in various ways to any layer.

What are paths good for? Consider the precision and editability of vector-based drawing and apply it to the concept of a selection. Now think of all the ways that selections can be used (and reused). In PhotoPlus, selections and paths are interchangeable.

In much the same way as layers in the Layers tab, independent paths are listed in the **Paths tab**, depicted with their own name and the **path outline** shown in the path's thumbnail.

There are two methods for creating a path. You can create:

- a path outline directly from drawn QuickShapes (see Path 2's Quick Star above) or outlines.

- a selection on your image from which the path outline can be created (see Path 3).

Either way, once you've got a path outline, you can reshape it (using the Outline tools), convert it to a selection, create a filled bitmap, or **stroke** a path—that is, draw the path onto a bitmap layer using the current brush. Paths are saved along with the image when you use the .SPP format.

To create a path outline from a QuickShape/outline or selection:

- Select a QuickShape and/or Outline tool, then ensure [icon] **Paths** is selected on the Context toolbar. (For details on using these tools, see Drawing and editing lines and shapes on p. 88).

- Drag across the page to create your path.
  OR

1. To create a path outline whose shape matches any selection area, first create the selection on a layer.

2. Click [icon] **Selection to Path** on the Paths tab.

3. In the dialog, choose a **Smoothness** setting (to even out jagged selections) and click **OK**. The new path outline appears on a new path with a default name (which you can change, as described below).

To duplicate the selected path and its outline:

- Right-click its name and choose **Duplicate Path**.

To delete the selected path:

- Click the Path tab's [icon] **Delete Path** button.

To rename the selected path:

1. Double-click its name.

2. In the dialog, type a new name for the path.

To edit a path outline:

- Use the **Node Edit Tool** to modify a path's shape by moving nodes or adjust outline curves by moving node handles.

- Use the **Shape Edit Tool** to move, resize, reshape, rotate, and skew the path by dragging the displayed bounding box handles in any direction.

For both methods, see Creating and editing outline shapes on p. 93 for more details.

You can also flip a path outline either horizontally or vertically. Use the **Flip Horizontally>Path** or **Flip Vertically>Path** option from the **Image** menu, respectively.

To create a selection from a path:

1. Select the Background or standard layer where you want to create the selection.

2. On the Paths tab, select the path from which you want to create the selection.

3. Click the [ ] **Path to Selection** button (or right-click the path entry).

4. In the dialog, set options for the selection:
   • The **Feather** value blurs the selection's edges by making edge pixels semi-transparent.
   • Check **Antialias** to produce smooth edges by softening the colour transition between edge pixels and background pixels.
   • Select **New Selection**, **Add to Selection**, **Subtract from Selection**, or **Intersect with Selection** to determine how the path-based selection should interact with an existing selection, if any.

5. Click **OK**. The selection marquee appears on the target layer.

To draw (stroke) a path onto a bitmap layer:

1. Select the Background or standard layer where you want to add the bitmap.

2. Choose a brush tool (such as the Paintbrush or Picture Brush) and set Colour, Brush Tip, and other properties from the Context toolbar.

3. On the Paths tab, select the path you want to stroke. Make sure the path is positioned where you want it.

4. Click the 🖌 **Stroke Path** button.

To create a filled bitmap from a path:

1. Select the Background or standard layer where you want to create the filled bitmap.

2. Set a foreground colour.

3. On the Paths tab, select the path you want to fill. Make sure the path is positioned where you want it.

4. Click the 🔷 **Fill Path** button (or right-click the path and choose **Fill Path**).

5

Image Adjustments and Effects

Introduction to image adjustments

A major part of photo-editing is making corrections (i.e., **adjustments**) to your own near-perfect images. Whether you've been snapping with your digital camera or you've just scanned a photograph, at some point you may need to call on PhotoPlus's powerful photo-correction tools to fix some unforeseen problems.

For photo-correction, several methods can be adopted. You can use a combination of:

- **Image colour adjustments**: For applying colour adjustments to a selection or layers.

- **QuickFix Studio**: For making cumulative corrective adjustments from within a studio environment.

- **Retouch** brush-based tools: Red Eye, Smudge, Blur, Sharpen, Dodge/Burn (for exposure control), Sponge (for saturation control), Scratch Remover.

If you work with raw images you can make image adjustments on your unprocessed raw file (before interpolation). Adjustments include **white balance**, **exposure**, **highlight recovery**, **noise reduction**, and **chromatic aberration** removal. See Opening a raw image on p. 21.

Overview: Adjusting image colours

PhotoPlus provides a number of different adjustment filters that you can apply to a selection or to an active standard layer. Typically, these adjustments are used to correct deficiencies in the original image. You can apply them either directly, via the **Image>Adjust** menu, or as an adjustment layer (see p. 143).

Each of the adjustment options works in a similar way. Alter the values by dragging on a slider, moving it to the left to decrease the value, or the right to increase the value, or enter a value in the field at the right of the slider.

> Instead of dragging the slider with the mouse, you can click on it and then jog it with the left or right keyboard arrow keys.

Here's a summary of the available PhotoPlus image adjustments (see PhotoPlus help for in-depth instructions).

- **AutoLevels** and **AutoContrast** redistribute the lightness (luminance) values in the image, making the darkest image pixel black and the lightest one white, and adjusting the spread in between. AutoLevels performs this adjustment separately for each of the Red, Green, and Blue channels, while AutoContrast operates on the image as a whole.

- **Levels** pops up a dialog that affords more precise levels control, along with AutoLevels and AutoContrast. While viewing a histogram plot of lightness values in the image, you can adjust the tonal range by shifting dark, light, and gamma values.

- **Curves** displays lightness values in the image using a line graph, and lets you adjust points along the curve to fine-tune the tonal range. AutoLevels and AutoContrast are also provided.

- **Colour Balance** lets you adjust colour and tonal balance for general colour correction in the image.

- **Brightness/Contrast**: Brightness refers to overall lightness or darkness, while contrast describes the tonal range, or spread between lightest and darkest values.

- **Shadow/Highlight/Midtone** controls the extent of shadows, highlights, and contrast within the image.

- **Hue/Saturation/Lightness**: Hue refers to the colour's tint—what most of us think of as rainbow or spectrum colours with name associations, like "blue" or "magenta." Saturation describes the colour's purity—a totally unsaturated image has only greys. Lightness is what we intuitively understand as relative darkness or lightness—ranging from full black at one end to full white at the other.

- **Replace Colour** lets you "tag" one or more ranges of the full colour spectrum that require adjustment in the image, then apply variations in hue, saturation, and/or brightness to just those colour regions (not to be confused with the simpler Replace Colour Tool).

- **Selective Colour** lets you add or subtract a certain percentage of cyan, magenta, yellow, and/or black ink for creating effects.

- **Channel Mixer** lets you modify a colour channel using a mix of the current colour channels.

- **Gradient Map** lets you remap greyscale (lightness) information in the image to a selected gradient. The function replaces pixels of a given lightness in the original image with the corresponding colour value from the gradient spectrum.

- **Lens Filter** adjusts the colour balance for warming or cooling down your photos. It digitally mimics the placement of a filter on the front of your camera lens.

- **Threshold** creates a monochromatic (black and white) rendering. You can set the threshold, i.e. the lightness or grey value above which colours are inverted.

- **Equalize** evenly distributes the lightness levels between existing bottom (darkest) and top (lightest) values.

- **Negative Image** inverts the colours, giving the effect of a photographic negative.

- **Black and White Film** is used for greyscale conversion with controllable source channel input.

- **Posterize** produces a special effect by reducing the image to a limited number of colours.

Besides the Brightness/Contrast adjustment, the PhotoPlus **Image** menu affords a number of functions you can apply to correct shadow/highlight values in an image. **Adjust>AutoLevels** or **Adjust>AutoContrast** may do the job in one go; if not, you can use **Adjust>Levels...** or **Adjust>Shadow/Highlight/Midtone...**.

> ★ Use the Histogram tab to display statistics and image colour values, helping you to evaluate the kinds of image adjustments that may be needed.

Using QuickFix Studio

The purpose of the **QuickFix Studio** is to provide an image **adjustment** environment within PhotoPlus which simplifies the often complicated process of image correction. You can consider QuickFix Studio as the image adjustment equivalent of PhotoPlus's Filter Gallery, which instead concentrates on applying and managing special effects.

An important feature is the ability to cumulatively apply adjustments (like applying filter gallery effects).

Let's get familiar with the QuickFix Studio's interface. The example used is of a wide-angle photo of an interesting building (the unwanted barrel distortion effect is being removed)—the non-default landscape dual-screen view is displayed.

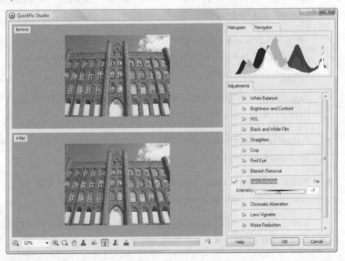

Adjustments are made available to the right of the main window (Lens Distortion is currently selected).

To launch QuickFix Studio:

- Click [🔍 QuickFix Studio] on the **Photo Studio** toolbar.

Adjustments overview

Here's a quick overview of all the adjustments hosted in QuickFix Studio:

- **White Balance**
  "Cool down" or "warm up" your photo by adjusting white balance either by selecting presets or customizing temperature/tint combinations.

- **Brightness and Contrast**
  Simple adjustments to a photo's exposure, brightness, contrast, shadows, and highlights.

- **HSL**
  Adjust the Hue, Saturation, and Lightness of your image independently.

- **Black and White Film**
  Intelligently apply greyscale by varying the grey tones of red, green or blue colours in your original image. Also apply colour tints.

- **Straighten**
  Re-aligns slightly or wildly crooked photos by resetting the image's horizon, then applying an auto-crop.

- **Crop**
  Retains a print-size portion of your image while discarding the remainder. Great for home printing, then framing. Optionally, size an unconstrained selection area to crop.

- **Red Eye**
  Removes the dreaded red eye effect from subject's eyes—commonly encountered with flash photography.

- **Blemish Removal**
  Removes simple skin blemishes and other flaws.

- **Lens Distortion**
  Fixes barrelling and pincushion distortion encountered when photographing straight-edged objects at close range.

- **Chromatic Aberration**
  Reduces red/cyan or blue/yellow fringing on object edges.

- **Lens Vignette**
  Removes darkening in photo corners.

- **Noise Reduction**
  Removes unwanted speckling in your photo.

- **Sharpen**
  Makes your image sharper at image edges—great for improving image quality after other adjustments have been made.

> ★ Some adjustments can also be applied independently from the **Effects** menu.

To apply an adjustment:

1. Click on the ▷ button adjacent to the chosen adjustment.

2. From the expanded adjustment options a selection of sliders, check boxes, and drop-down menus can be modified (you can also enter absolute values into available input boxes). Whatever settings are changed, the image will be adjusted automatically to reflect the new settings in the preview window.

   Click on the ▽ button to collapse the adjustment options once finished with (leaving space for further adjustments).

An adjustment is applied if a ⬅ button appears at the end of the adjustment entry (click the button to remove the adjustment completely). If you want to temporarily hide an adjustment, click on the ✓ **Show/Hide** button at the start of the adjustment entry; your settings will be remembered when you switch the adjustment back on.

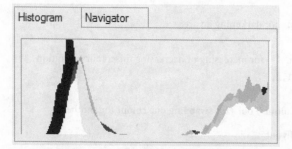

💡 When increasing the Exposure value, use the histogram to check that your highlights aren't clipped (i.e., when the graph disappears abruptly off the right-hand edge of the histogram).

Retouching

The **Tools** toolbar includes an assortment of comparatively simple brush-based tools that come in handy at various stages of photo editing. For the most part the tools are hosted on the Retouch Tools flyout, but the blemish, scratch and patch removal tools exist on the Repair Tools flyout.

Retouching tools work on Background and standard layers, but not on text layers or shape layers.

On the Retouch Tools flyout:

Red Eye Tool - for correcting the "red eye" phenomenon common in colour snapshots

Smudge Tool - for picking up colour from the click point and "pushing" it in the brush stroke direction

Blur Tool - for reducing contrast under the brush, softening edges without smearing colours

Sharpen Tool - for increasing contrast under the brush, enhancing apparent sharpness

Dodge Tool - for lightening an area

Burn Tool - for darkening an area

 Sponge Tool - - for increasing or decreasing the colour saturation under the brush

 Replace Colour Tool - for swapping one colour for another

On the Repair Tool flyout:

 Blemish Remover - for intelligently painting out skin blemishes

Scratch Remover - for filling in small gaps or dropouts in an image

Patch Tool - for painting out selected areas

Overview: Applying special effects

Creative effects are grouped into different categories, i.e. **distortion**, **blur**, **sharpen**, **edge**, **noise**, **render**, and **stylistic**. Individual effects can be applied to the active layer or selection either individually or cumulatively via a Filter Gallery. As with image adjustments (see Overview: adjusting image colours on p. 106), you can use filter effects to improve the image, for example by sharpening, but more often the emphasis here is on the "creative" possibilities when effects are applied.

Equally dramatic artistic effects can be applied by using the studio-based Instant Artist, warp tools via the **Tools** toolbar's flyout, or 2D/3D layer effects via the Layers tab.

Instant Artist effects

Instant Artist will bring your artistic side out—creating your own masterpieces by picking from a variety of classic painting styles (with no paint splashes!). The tool will transform your image in a single-click. Classic styles include Expressionist, Impressionist, Oil, Old Master, and many others. More abstract styles are available such as Munchist and Van Gogh.

Whichever style you choose, you can take advantage of Instant Artist's powerful studio environment. This provides a resizable dialog with large scale preview window, a thumbnail gallery showing each effect (for visual clues), and a comprehensive range of context-sensitive effect settings. Instant Artist's interruptible redraw also means that you can make changes to your settings without waiting for your image to refresh; the effect will be redrawn immediately.

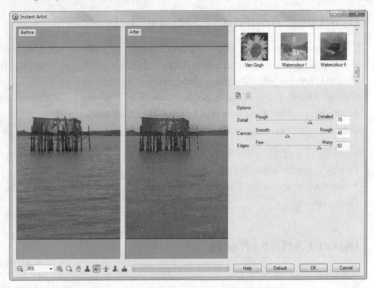

To launch Instant Artist:

1. Click the **Instant Artist** button on the **Photo Studio** toolbar (or select the option from the **Effects** menu).

2. Select an effect's thumbnail from the thumbnail pane. You'll see your image update to reflect the new effect.

3. To see a different part of the image, drag it with the hand cursor. Click the Zoom buttons to zoom in or out.

4. Adjust the sliders (or enter specific values) to vary the effect. If necessary, click the **Default** button to revert to the standard settings for this effect.

5. To save the current settings as a custom style you can use later, click the **Add Style** button and provide a name for the new style. The new style appears in the thumbnail pane. (To delete a style you've added, select its thumbnail and click the **Delete Style** button.)

6. Click **OK** to apply the effect, or **Cancel** to abandon changes.

For more details, search for Instant Artist in the PhotoPlus Help index.

Warp tool effects

The entries on the Warp Tools flyout work as a group. Most of them shift pixels that the brush passes over, while the last one undoes the cumulative effects of the others. The actual amount of pixel displacement depends on the direction of brush movement, the brush tip, and the Context toolbar's Opacity, Brush Size, and Quality settings.

The **Elastic Warp Tool** shifts pixels in the direction of brush motion, hence the appearance of pulling or elasticity.

The **Pinch** and **Punch Tools** apply, respectively, a concave or convex spherical distortion under the brush. To apply this effect to a selection or layer, use **Effects>Distort>Pinch/Punch...**.

The **Twirl Tools** produce a "spin art" effect—liquid paint on a surface revolving either clockwise or anti-clockwise around a central point. As with Pinch and Punch, you can apply either effect to a selection or layer using the **Effects>Distort>Twirl**.

The **Thick/Thin Warp Tool** shifts pixels 90° to the right of the brush direction, which has the effect of spreading or compressing edges along the stroke.

The **Unwarp Tool** reduces the strength of the current warped effect under the brush.

Applying 2D layer effects

Layer effects can be applied to the contents of standard (transparent) layers, text layers, or shape layers. Standard or "2D" layer effects like shadow, glow, bevel, and emboss are particularly well adapted to text, while 3D layer effects (covered elsewhere; p. 118) create the impression of a textured surface.

Unlike image adjustments and **Effects** menu manipulations, layer effects don't directly change image pixels—they work like mathematical "lenses" that transform how a layer's bitmap appears. Since the settings are independent, you can adjust them ad infinitum until you get the result you want!

Here's an example of each effect applied to the letter "A".

Drop Shadow   Inner Shadow   Outer Glow   Inner Glow

Inner Bevel   Outer Bevel   Emboss   Pillow Emboss

Colour Fill   Outline

- **Drop Shadow** adds a diffused shadow "behind" solid regions on a layer.

- **Inner Shadow** adds a diffused shadow effect inside the edge of an object.

- **Outer Glow** adds a colour border outside the edge of an object.

- **Inner Glow** filter adds a colour border inside the edge of an object.

- Bevel and Emboss/**Inner Bevel** adds a rounded-edge effect inside an object.

- Bevel and Emboss/**Outer Bevel** adds a rounded-edge effect (resembling a drop shadow) outside an object.

- Bevel and Emboss/**Emboss** adds a convex rounded edge and shadow effect to an object.

- Bevel and Emboss/**Pillow Emboss** adds a concave rounded edge and shadow effect to an object.

- **Colour Fill** lets you apply a specific colour to a layer.

- **Outline** applies a border effect to the edge of an object. See Creating outlines on p. 96.

To apply a shadow, glow, bevel, or emboss effect:

1. From the Layers tab, select a layer and click ⚡ **Add Layer Effects**.

2. In the dialog, apply an effect by checking its check box in the list at left. You can apply multiple effects to the layer.

3. To adjust the properties of a specific effect, select its name and adjust the dialog controls. Adjust the sliders, drop-down menu, or enter specific values to vary each effect. Options differ from one effect to another.

Drop Shadow

Blend Mode:	Multiply ▾		
Opacity:	△		75
Blur:	△		5
Distance:	△		5
Intensity:	△		0
Colour:	▮		
Angle:	◕	45	

4.   Click **OK** to apply the effect or **Cancel** to abandon changes.

Applying 3D layer effects

3D layer effects are just as easy to apply, but they're a bit more complex than their 2D cousins (see p. 116). Actually, there's an easy way to get started with them: simply display the **Instant Effects tab** and preview its gallery thumbnails.

In the tab you'll see a variety of remarkable 3D surface and texture presets grouped into wide-ranging "themed" categories (e.g., Glass Text, Abstract, Wood, Metal, etc.). Click any thumbnail to apply it to the active layer. Assuming the layer has some colour on it to start with, you'll see an instant result!

Instant Effects

Scale % △ 100

Category Abstract ▾

To apply an Instant Effects tab preset to the active layer: :

- Display the **Instant Effects** tab and select a category, then click a gallery thumbnail.

- To make the effect appear smaller or larger in relation to the image, drag the **Scale** slider or type a value in the tab.

You can apply an effect from the Instant Effects tab preset, edit it (using the Layer Effects dialog) and then save it as a custom preset in a user-defined category (you'll have to create and select the category first). To save the preset, right-click in the tab and choose **Add Item....** From the dialog, you can adjust the Scale of the effect and have your thumbnail preview stored as a Rectangle or as Text (using the letter "A"). For either type, the thumbnail will appear in the gallery.

⚡ If you want to have complete flexibility when creating 3D effects, you can click the **Add Layer Effects** button on the Layers tab. The dialog is shared for both 2D and 3D effects—simply check the 3D Effects box and experiment with the settings (enable other 3D check boxes as appropriate).

3D effects overview

✔ 3D Effects
   3D Bump Map
      Function
         Advanced
   2D Bump Map
✔ 3D Pattern Map
      Function
         Advanced
   2D Pattern Map
   Reflection Map
   Transparency
✔ 3D Lighting

Suppose you've applied a 3D layer effect preset from the Instant Effects tab, and then you bring up the Layer Effects dialog. On inspecting the settings used in the preset, the first thing you'll notice is that three boxes may be checked.

- **3D Effects** is a master switch for this group, and its settings of **Blur** and **Depth** make a great difference; you can click the "+" button to unlink them for independent adjustment.

- **3D Pattern Map** allows for blend mode, opacity, depth, displacement and softening adjustments, along with a choice of gradient fills. This is checked depending on the type of instant effect selected.

• **3D Lighting** provides a "light source" without which any depth information in the effect wouldn't be visible. The lighting settings let you illuminate your 3D landscape and vary its reflective properties.

Another thing you'll probably wonder about is that all the 3D effects seem to have "map" in their name. The concept of a **map** is the key to understanding how these effects work: it means a channel of information overlaid on the image, storing values for each underlying image pixel. You can think of the layer as a picture printed on a flexible sheet, which is flat to start with. Each 3D layer effect employs a map that interacts with the underlying image on a layer to create the visual impression of a textured surface.

Bump Maps superimpose depth information for a bumpy, peak-and-valley effect. Using the flexible sheet metaphor, the bump map adds up-and-down contours and the image "flexes" along with these bumps, like shrink-wrap, while a light from off to one side accentuates the contours.

Pattern Maps contribute colour variations using a choice of blend modes and opacity, for realistic (or otherworldly!) depictions of wood grain, marbling, and blotches or striations of all kinds.

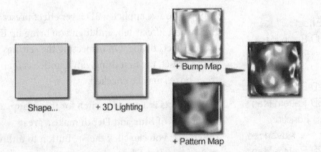

Shape...   + 3D Lighting   + Bump Map

+ Pattern Map

You'll notice that Bump Maps and Pattern Maps come in two varieties: "2D" and "3D." Don't confuse these with the "2D layer effects" (like Drop Shadow). The map-based effects are all three-dimensional effects—the distinction in name has to do with how each one achieves its result. Here's the difference: With the "3D" Bump Maps and Pattern Maps, you first pick a mathematical function. With the "2D map" variants, you begin by selecting a bitmap from a gallery.

The function-based maps include data about the interior of the "space," while the bitmap-based maps describe only surface characteristics.

You'll see this distinction more clearly if you experiment with **depth maps**, as covered in Using depth maps (see p. 152). Depth maps create extra depth to your image, by adding an extra channel (storing Z-axis or depth information). As a result, contoured surfaces are possible which are exposed by applied 3D layer effects.

Transparency

The uniform transparency of a layer and its objects (with 3D layer effects applied) can be controlled via the Layers tab with the Opacity option (see rear heart shape in example below). However, for more sophisticated transparency control, transparency settings can instead be set within the Layer Effects dialog. The effect can be used to create more realistic transparency by independently controlling transparency on reflective (edges) and non-reflective (flat) areas of the object (see front heart shape below).

> Use this effect in conjunction with reflection maps and multiple directional light sources for ultra-realistic glass effects.

3D Lighting + Layer
Opacity 50%

3D Lighting +
Transparency
effect

3D Reflection Map

The **3D Reflection Map** effect is used to simulate mirrored surfaces by selection of a pattern (i.e., a bitmap which possesses a shiny surface) which "wraps around" a selected object. Patterns which simulate various realistic indoor and outdoor environments can be adopted, with optional use of 3D lighting to further reflect off object edges.

Using the Filter Gallery

The Filter Gallery offers a one-stop shop for applying **single** or **multiple** filter effects. The gallery hosts sets of filter thumbnails which are categorized into different effect categories (e.g., Distort, Blur, Sharpen, Edge, Noise, Render). Thumbnails are shown in expandable categories (see Distort filter effects below); each thumbnail is a sample of your currently active image with the relevant filter effect applied.

It's possible to apply several filter effects to the same image within the Filter Gallery, and, depending on the order in which they are applied, to end up with a different final result. In the above example, the Ripple and Unsharp Mask effects are sequentially applied.

If you would like to manage your filter effects (swap, modify or delete any previously applied effect) at a later date, you can apply filter effects on a special Filter Layer (see p. 146). Otherwise the filter effect is permanently applied to the layer.

To further extend creative possibilities, you can create your own **custom** filter effects within the Filter Gallery (see PhotoPlus Help for more information) or adopt third-party Photoshop plug-ins (see p. 126).

To view the Filter Gallery:

- Click the [🎨 Filter Gallery] button on the **Photo Studio** toolbar. No
  effect filter loaded.
  OR

- To make a Filter Layer, right-click a standard or Background layer in
  the Layers tab, and choose **Convert to Filter Layer....** (See Using filter
  layers on p. 146.)

You can add to any effect by creating a stack where additional effects can be
added and built up. Any effect can then be switched on/off, deleted or reordered
in this list. In addition, you can easily swap one effect for another, especially
useful if you want to preserve the order of other applied effects.

> Selecting a filter effect directly from the **Effects** menu will
> automatically launch the Filter Gallery with the effect already
> applied.

To add a filter in the Filter Gallery:

1. Expand your chosen effect category by clicking the ▷ **Expand**
   button. You'll see effect thumbnails representing how your image will
   look if the effect is applied.

2. Click on an effect thumbnail to apply it to your image (or right-click
   and choose **Add Filter**).
   OR

   Choose the [➕ Add Filter] button, selecting your filter effect from the
   flyout menu.

   The applied filter is shown in a filter stack in the lower-right corner of
   the Filter Gallery. The large preview window updates as you adjust any
   filter properties' sliders or enter new values.

To add further filter effects, use the [➕ Add Filter] button again, right-click
another effect thumbnail (choosing **Add Filter**), or just **Alt**-click on the
thumbnail.

Clicking a thumbnail will replace any currently selected filter in your filter stack.

To switch a filter on or off:

- To switch a selected filter effect off, click the icon next to its name in the Filter Stack. The icon changes to a closed eye. Click again to switch on.

  As an example, a click on the Diffuse Glow filter (below) will hide the effect, but clicking the Paper Cutout's closed eye icon will make the filter visible.

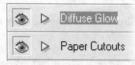

The effect's properties are displayed by default but can be collapsed to make more of your effects stack visible.

To collapse/expand filter properties:

- To collapse, click the ▽ button preceding the filter effect name. To expand again, click the ▷ button.

The properties of any selected effect will be displayed in the expanded area under the effect name—you can alter and experiment with these at any time.

To modify a filter:

- Select the filter you wish to modify, expanding the filter entry to view properties if needed (click the ▷ button).

- Change properties by enabling/disabling radio buttons or check boxes, and adjusting sliders. Alternatively, enter values into input boxes.

- Use the **Undo** button to undo recent changes to the filter (or the **Redo** button to re-apply the changes).

To replace a filter:

1. Select the filter you wish to replace by clicking its name.

2. Pick an effect gallery, then click a filter effect's thumbnail as a replacement (or right-click then choose **Replace Filter**). Your selected filter is replaced in the stack with no change made to the existing stack order.

The order in which effects appear in the effect list may produce very different results. If you're not happy with the current order, PhotoPlus lets you drag and drop your effects into any position in the stack. Effects are applied in the same way that layers are applied, i.e. the first effect applied always appears at the bottom of the list and is applied to the photo first.

However, filters can be moved around the filter list to change the order in which they are applied to the photo.

> ★ Alt-clicking on a thumbnail will add a new filter effect instead of replacing your selected filter effect.

To reorder filters:

1. Select the filter you wish to reorder.

2. Drag the filter's name to another position in the list. A red line indicates the new position in which the filter will be placed if the mouse button is released.

Using plug-ins

PhotoPlus supports **non-automated** Adobe Photoshop-compatible plug-in filters. Any such industry-standard filters located in your PhotoPlus Plugins folder will appear on the **Effects** menu.

> ★ Due to the varying standard of third-party plug-ins, you may experience problems when using this feature. This is beyond Serif's control, so we recommend that you save your work before using plug-ins, and then test your plug-ins before commencing.

To apply a plug-in filter:

- Choose it from **Effects>Plugin Filters**. Either the effect will be applied immediately, or the plug-in will display its own dialog.

To check or change the plug-in filter folder:

1. Choose **Preferences...** from the **File** menu and select the **Plugins** tab. Initially the dialog shows the path you selected during installation.

2. To change the designated folder, click the **Browse...** button and use the dialog to locate the correct folder.
   OR

   Create Windows shortcuts within the folder, pointing to the plug-ins stored outside the PhotoPlus Plugins folder.

Merging bracketed photos

High Dynamic Range (HDR) merge, or tone mapping, is used to combine bracketed photos or scanned images from film, each shot taken at different exposure levels (typically one each for highlights, midtones, and shadows) and within seconds apart. Your camera can't capture all exposure levels in a single shot, so by bringing together multiple photos you can expand your image's dynamic range which would otherwise be impossible in a single shot.

Typically, scenes of high contrast such as landscapes, sunsets or indoor environments (with strong lighting) are suited to HDR Merge.

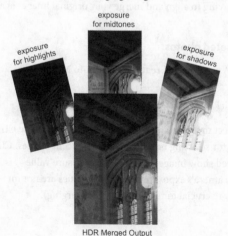

exposure
for midtones

exposure
for highlights

exposure
for shadows

HDR Merged Output

For good results, it's important to bear the following points in mind:

- Many modern cameras offer **auto-bracketing** which automatically takes several shots at different exposure levels. A two-EV spacing is considered to be optimum for most occasions. Alternatively, shoot with manual exposure set.

- Always shoot the same scene! Your output is based on a composite of the same scene.

- Take as many shots as is needed to cover your required dynamic range.

- Use a tripod for optimum camera stability. Also avoid photographing objects affected by windy conditions (e.g., moving tree branches).

- Ensure **Aperture priority** is set on your camera (see your camera's operating manual for more details).

The HDR merge is a two-stage process, firstly to select the source files (JPG or raw) for merging, and then performing the merge itself after having adjusted merge settings to optimize the output). The process can be carried out directly on source files without loading them into your project in advance.

PhotoPlus lets you optionally save the merged HDR image to one of several formats (namely OpenEXR, HDR and HD Photo), which can be opened at a later date, saving you from having to align and merge your original images again (see p. 19).

To select and merge bracketed photos:

1. From the Startup Wizard, click **Create>HDR Photo Merge.**

2. From the dialog, click ⬚ Add ⬚.

3. Browse to, then select multiple files from the chosen folder—use **Ctrl**-click or **Shift**-click for selecting non-adjacent or adjacent images. Click **Open**. The files listed show image name and an exposure value equivalent to your camera's exposure setting (the values are not for just for show—they're crucial for successful HDR merging).

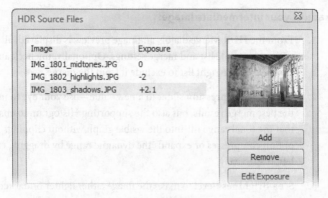

Click the **Add** button to add more photos or the **Remove** button to exclude a selected photo.

For scanned images (from camera film) which won't possess EXIF-derived Exposure values, you can click the **Edit Exposure** button to add your own exposure values if you've kept a record (or you could just add +2.0, 0, and -2 then experiment with the results).

4. (Optional) Uncheck **Align images** if you're sure your source images are perfectly aligned (perhaps by a third-party application). Otherwise, PhotoPlus will automatically attempt to align each photo's corresponding pixel data.

5. (Optional) Check **Infer film response curve** to affect a tone curve needed to accurately process scanned images (from camera film). Otherwise, keep unchecked for digital camera use.

6. Click **OK**. The Merge HDR dialog is displayed, showing a preview of your intermediate HDR image.

★ Don't worry if your initial results look less than desirable. You're only half way towards your stunning image but you'll need to modify the HDR image using a series of adjustments.

To adjust your intermediate image:

1. From the HDR Merge dialog, an image preview is displayed, along with a merge file list and merge settings. Optionally, uncheck an image from the upper-right list to exclude it from the merge.

2. Drag the **Compression** slider to a new value—use your eye to judge the best merge results, but also the supporting Histogram to ensure that the tonal range fits into the visible graph without clipping. The option compresses or expands the dynamic range by dragging right or left, respectively.

3. Set a **Brightness** level to make the image either lighter or darker.

4. Adjust the **Black Point** slider right to shift the histogram's left-most edge making all affected pixels in the shadow region turn black.

5. Reduce **Local Contrast Radius** to alleviate image "flatness" when compressing the dynamic range (see Compression above).

6. Set the **Temperature** to give a warmer "reddish" or cooler "blueish" look; drag to the right or left, respectively.

7. Adjust the **Saturation** value to reduce or boost the colour in your image.

8. Check **Output 16-bits per channel** if you're looking for the highest level of detail in your merged output.

9. Click **OK**.

10. From the next dialog, you'll be asked if you want to save the intermediate HDR Image or just continue as an untitled project.

    - Click **Yes** to preserve the HDR image. This saves having to select, align, and merge images again, but you'll still need to reapply any adjustments previously made. Select a file location, file format, name for your file, then click **Save**. The file format (OpenEXR .exr, Radiance .hdr, or HD Photo .hdp) can be chosen from the drop-down menu.
      OR

- Click **No** if you don't need to preserve the HDR image (you'll have to select, align, and merge again). Your merge results will be the basis for an Untitled project.

★ If you've created an intermediate HDR image, it can be opened as for any other file (see p. 19).

6
Layers and Masks

Layers and Masks

Basics of using layers

If you're accustomed to thinking of pictures as flat illustrations in books, or as photographic prints, the concept of **image layers** may take some getting used to. In fact, layers are hardly unique to electronic images. The emulsion of photographic film has separate layers, each sensitive to a different colour—and we've all noticed multiple-image depth effects like shop window reflections or mirrored interiors. There is still something magical about being able to build up an image in a series of planes, like sheets of electronic glass, each of which can vary in transparency and interact with the layers below to produce exciting new images and colours.

Kinds of layers

In a typical PhotoPlus image—for example, a photograph you've scanned in, a new picture file you've just created, or a standard bitmap file you've opened—there is one layer that behaves like a conventional "flat" image. This is called the **Background layer**, and you can think of it as having paint overlaid on an opaque, solid colour surface.

You can create any number of new layers in your image. Each new one appears on top of the currently active layer, comprising a stack that you can view and manipulate with the Layers tab. We call these additional layers **standard layers** to differentiate them from the Background layer. Standard layers such as "Surfer Girl" and "Beach" opposite behave like transparent sheets through which the underlying layers are visible.

Other types of layers also exist in PhotoPlus:

- **Shape layers** are specifically designed to keep drawn lines and shapes (including QuickShapes) separate from the other layers so that they remain editable. (See Drawing and editing lines and shapes; p. 88)

- **Text layers**, work like Shape layers, but are intended exclusively for Text. (See Creating and editing text; p. 86)

- **Adjustment layers** apply corrective image adjustments to lower layers. (See Using adjustment layers; p. 143)

- **Filter layers**, are much like standard layers, but you can apply one or more filter effects to the layer without permanently altering layer content. You also have full control over effects in the future. (See Using filter layers; p. 146)

For now though we're concerned mainly with the Background and standard layers. .

A key distinction is that pixels on the Background layer are always opaque, while those on standard layers can vary in opacity (or transparency—another way of expressing the same property). That's because standard layers have a "master" Opacity setting that you can change at any time (with on-screen real-time preview), while the Background layer does not. A couple of examples will show how this rule is applied in PhotoPlus:

- Suppose you are creating a new image. The New Image dialog provides three choices for Background: White, Background Colour, and Transparent. If you pick White or Background Colour, the Layers tab shows a single layer in the new image named "Background." If you pick Transparent, however, the single layer is named "Layer 1"—and in this case, the image (typically an animation file) has no Background layer.

- If you cut, delete, or move a selection on the Background layer, the "hole" that's left exposes the current background colour (as shown on the Colour tab). The same operations on a standard layer expose a transparent hole.

Selections and layers

With few exceptions, you will work on just one layer at any given time, clicking in the Layers tab to select the current or **active layer**. Selections and layers are related concepts. Whenever there's a selection, certain tools and commands operate only on the pixels inside the selection—as opposed to a condition where nothing is selected, in which case those functions generally affect the entire active layer.

If your image has multiple layers, and you switch to another layer, the selection doesn't stay on the previous layer—it follows you to the new active layer. This makes sense when you realize that the selection doesn't actually include image content—it just describes a region with boundaries. And following the old advice "Don't confuse the map with the territory," you can think of the selection as a kind of outline map, and the active layer as the territory.

Operations involving layers

Many standard operations, such as painting, selecting and moving, Clipboard actions, adjusting colours, applying effects, and so on, are possible on both the Background layer and standard layers.

Others, such as rearranging the order of layers in the stack, setting up different colour interactions (blend modes and blend ranges) between layers, varying layer opacity (transparency), applying 2D layer effects and 3D layer effects, using depth maps, creating animation frames, or masking, only work with standard layers.

Once an image has more than just a background layer, the layer information can only be preserved by saving the image in the native PhotoPlus (.SPP) format. Multiple layers are **merged** when you export an image to a standard "flat" bitmap format (e.g., .PNG). It's best to save your work-in-progress as .SPP files, and only export to a different file format as the final step.

Some standard operations can be applied to all layers simultaneously by checking the **Use All Layers** option from the Context toolbar.

To carry out basic layer operations:

- To select a layer, click on its name in the Layers tab. The selected layer is now the **active layer**. Note that each layer's entry includes a preview thumbnail, which is visible at all times and is especially useful when identifying layer contents.

- To select multiple layers together, use **Ctrl**-click or **Shift**-click to select non-adjacent or adjacent layers in the tab's stack. Once selected, multiple layers can be moved, linked, aligned, duplicated, grouped, rearranged, hidden, merged and deleted. To select all layers, choose **Select All layers** from the **Layers** menu, or for just linked layers, choose **Select Linked Layers**.

- To create a new standard layer above the active layer, click the New Layer button on the Layers tab. Dragging a file icon and dropping it onto the current window also creates a new layer from the dragged image.

- Select [icon] **New Layer Group** to create a group in which you can store layers which have some relationship to each other—some layers may only be related to a specific photo feature such that any changes to those layers will be restricted to the group's scope only. This gives greater control to enable changes to opacity, blend modes and hide/show layer settings for the group rather than for individual layers.

- Click the [icon] **New Adjustment Layer** button to apply an image adjustment to a layer (See Using adjustment layers on p. 143).

- The [icon] **Add Layer Mask** button adds a mask to the currently selected layer.

- The [icon] **Add Layer Depth Map** button creates a depth map for the selected layer.

- The [icon] **Add Layer Effects** button creates a 2D or 3D effect on the layer. Right-click to copy/paste, clear or hide effects.

- To remove one or more selected layers, click the [icon] **Delete Layer** button on the Layers tab. Hidden layers can also be deleted without prior selection by using **Delete>Hidden Layers**. (You can delete the Background layer, as long as it's not the only layer.)

- [icon] To make a layer's contents visible or invisible, click the **Hide/Show Layer** button next to its name on the Layers tab. The icon switches between an open and closed eye.

- Use [icons] lock buttons on the Layers tab to prevent accidental modification of opacity, pixel colour, object positions or all three on the active layer (or group), respectively.

- To convert any shape or text layer to a standard layer, right-click on the layer name and choose **Rasterize** from the menu.

- Use different thumbnail sizes in the Layers tab by clicking the ▷ **Tab Menu** button, then choosing **Small Thumbnails** or **Large Thumbnails**.

- To convert the Background layer to a standard (transparent) layer, right-click "Background" on the Layers tab and choose **Promote to Layer**. The layer's name changes from "Background" to "Layer <number>." To convert a standard layer to a Background layer, right-click the layer and choose **Layer to Background**.

- To access Layer Properties—including Name, Blend Mode, Opacity, and Blend Ranges—right-click the layer name and choose **Properties**....

To control layer content:

- To select all layer content use **Select>Select All** or **Ctrl+A**. To select non-transparent regions on a layer, **Ctrl**-click on a layer thumbnail. Use **Invert** to selection transparent regions.

- ⊕ To move layer content, select one or more layers containing the content to be moved (from the Layers tab), then drag with the **Move Tool** with no selection area present (press **Ctrl+D** to remove any selection).

- To align layer content, select one or more layers (as above), then choose **Align** from the **Layers** menu, then select an option from the submenu.

- To distribute layer content, select one or more layers (as above), then choose **Distribute** from the **Layers** menu, then select an option from the submenu.

To carry out advanced layer operations:

- To create a new standard layer from a selection, choose **New Layer from Selection Copy** or **New Layer from Selection Cut** from the **Layers** menu. The former command leaves the original region intact; the latter cuts the original region to the Clipboard.

- To clone one or more active layers and their contents as new standard layers, right-click the selected layers then choose **Duplicate...** (or **Alt**-drag in the editing window with Move Tool selected) . The process also lets you copy the layer to a new or currently opened image.

- To link layers, select multiple layers and choose **Link Layers** from the **Layers** menu (or right-click in the Layers tab).

- To rearrange layers, select the layer(s) in the Layers tab and drag up or down. A red line "drop target" appears between layers as you drag. Drop the layer(s) on a target to relocate in the stack.

- To merge layers together into one, right click and choose **Merge Down** (merges into layer below), **Merge Visible** (merges only visible layers), **Merge Selected Layers** (merges currently selected layers), or **Merge All** (to flatten all layers into one).

Using layer groups

For greater management and efficiency it is possible to place selected layers into a pre-defined group, created with the **New Layer Group** button in the Layers tab.

In the example opposite, the highlighted "Beach Only" group contains two transparent standard layers called "Beach" and "Surfer Girl".

Alternatively, you can select multiple layers and add them to a new unnamed group by selecting either **New Layer Group from Selected Layers** or **Group Layers** on the **Layers** menu. There are many reasons why you might want to use groups in addition to layers. Here are a few...

- To create a self-contained group of layers which are all related, e.g. all the Text Layers used in your photo.

- To collect layers together which make up a specific photo feature, e.g. the beach components of a seaside shot.

- To make a mask or blend apply to only specific layers, i.e. those that contained within a group.

- To apply changes to a group that you would otherwise have to apply to each layer in turn—thus improving efficiency.

In reality a group is really just another layer but one which can store layers within itself. It's not surprising then that a group can have its own blend mode, opacity and blend ranges just like a layer. A group can also be merged and made visible/invisible—or even grouped within another group.

To create a Layer Group:

- Select a layer to set the position in the layer stack in which you want to place the Layer Group.

- Choose the ⬜ **New Layer Group** button (or select **New Layer Group...** from the **Layers** menu).

- In the dialog, enter group name, blend mode, opacity, and blend range for the group.

- Click **OK**.

To add one or more layers to a Layer Group:

- Select the layer(s) you want to add to the group and drag onto the group name. The layer(s) will then appear indented under the group.

To remove a layer:

- To remove the layer(s), drag the layer away from the group and drop it into an ungrouped area of the Layers tab (a red line indicate where the layer is to be placed). You can also use **Ungroup Layers** from the **Layers** menu if all layers are to be removed.

To merge a Layer Group:

- To flatten the layer group, select the group and choose **Merge>Merge Layer Group** from the **Layers** menu.

★ You cannot move the Background layer to a group.

Using adjustment layers

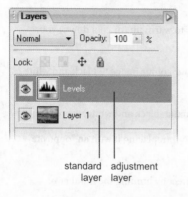

standard adjustment
layer layer

Adjustment layers let you insert any number of image adjustments experimentally. Unlike the other layer types, adjustment layers don't store content in the form of bitmap images, text, or shapes. Rather, an adjustment layer applies the adjustment to content on **all** layers below it (you can restrict the effects of the adjustment to one underlying layer by adding both to a group; see p. 141).

Adjustment layers all have corresponding entries on the **Image** menu—but instead of altering the image or layer directly as with the **Image>Adjust** commands, adjustment layers let you revisit the settings for a given adjustment as often as needed, while continuing to edit the image in other ways. If you later decide you don't even need an adjustment, you can simply remove it!

The following adjustments are available as adjustment layers:

- **Levels:** Adjust contrast and tonal range by shifting dark, light, and mid-tone values.

- **Curves:** Fine-tune lightness (luminance) values in the image or colour channel using a line graph.

- **Colour Balance:** Adjust colour and tonal balance for general colour correction in the image.

- **Brightness/Contrast:** Vary brightness and/or contrast.

- **Hue/Saturation/Lightness:** Vary hue, saturation, and/or lightness values, or colourize an image.

- **Selective Colour:** Add or subtract a certain percentage of cyan, magenta, yellow, and/or black ink.

- **Channel Mixer:** Modify a colour channel using a mix of the current colour channels.

- **Gradient Map:** Remap greyscale (lightness) information in the image to a selected gradient.

- **Lens Filter**: Apply a colour filter to warm up (or cool down) your image.

- **Black & White Film**: Convert your colour image to black and white intelligently.

- **Threshold:** Create a monochromatic (black and white) representation.

- **Negative Image:** Invert each colour, replacing it with an "opposite" value.

- **Posterize:** Apply the Posterize effect by limiting the number of lightness levels.

For more in-depth details on each adjustment, view the PhotoPlus help, click the Contents tab, and open the "Image Adjustments and Effects" book.

To create an adjustment layer:

1. Click the ⬤ **New Adjustment Layer** button on the Layers tab.

2. Select the name of the adjustment from the flyout menu.

Levels..
Curves...
Colour Balance...
Brightness/Contrast...
Hue/Saturation/Lightness...
Selective Colour...
Channel Mixer...
Gradient Map...
Lens Filter...
Black and White Film...
Threshold...
Negative Image
Posterize...

3. Use the displayed dialog to pick the settings to be applied, then click **OK**. A new adjustment layer, with adjustment name and identifying thumbnail, is inserted above the active layer. The adjustment is applied to all underlying layers.

To change the specific settings for an effect:

- Double-click the adjustment layer's name in the list and then use the dialog again.

To access layer properties for an adjustment layer:

- Right-click the layer name and choose **Properties**....

As with other layers, you can change the adjustment layer's name, hide the adjustment, set its Opacity, Blend Mode and/or Blend Ranges. You can also drag an adjustment layer up or down within the Layers tab to determine exactly which other layers are below and therefore affected by it.

Using filter layers

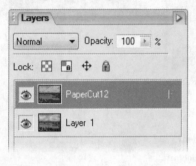

If you apply a filter effect to a standard or background layer, the layer is permanently altered. However, if you want the flexibility of being able to edit your filter effects at any point in the future (and don't want to destroy the layer contents) you can create a **Filter Layer** (e.g., PaperCut12) directly over your standard or background layer.

This non-destructive approach keeps layer content independent of your effects. Otherwise without filter layers, you would have to repeatedly undo your operations if you've had a rethink and no longer want to apply a specific layer's filter effect.

When a Filter Layer is created, the Filter Gallery is launched which allows one or more of your chosen filter effects to be added. At any point in the future, you can control your effects from the Filter Gallery—add, modify, replace, or delete effects equally!

To convert to a filter layer:

1. In the Layers tab, right-click a standard or Background layer and choose **Convert to Filter Layer...**.

2. From the displayed Filter Gallery, open a filter category (e.g. Distort, Blur, etc.) by clicking the ▽ button, then choose a filter thumbnail (showing a preview of your image with the filter applied).

    See Using the Filter Gallery on p. 123 for more details.

3. Click **OK** to close the Filter Gallery. The layer now shows the letter "F" indicating that one or more filter effects are now applied.

To edit the filter layer:

-   In the Layers tab, double-click the filter layer.

-   From the Filter Gallery, add, modify, or delete filter effects, then click **OK**. The changes are stored in the modified Filter Layer.

Using blend modes

You can think of **blend modes** as different rules for putting pixels together to create a resulting colour. In PhotoPlus, you'll encounter blend modes in several contexts:

-   As a property of individual **tools**, the tool's blend mode determines what happens if you use the tool to apply a new colour pixel on top of an existing colour pixel. Note that once you've applied paint to a region, that's it— you've changed the colour of pixels there. Subsequently changing a tool's blend mode won't alter brush strokes you've already laid down!

    Behind and Clear modes are only available for tools and not for layers.

- As a property of individual **layers**, a layer's blend mode determines how each pixel on that layer visibly combines with those on layers below. (Because there are no layers below the Background layer, it can't have a blend mode.) Note that changing a layer's blend mode property doesn't actually alter the pixels on the layer—so you can create different blend mode effects after creating the image content, then merge layers when you've achieved the result you want.

- As a property of certain 3D layer effects, where the blend mode is one of many settings that determine a colour change superimposed on the layer's pixels. The effects themselves are editable and don't alter the actual pixel values—nor does the effect's blend mode alter the layer's blend mode setting.

For an illustration of the individual blend modes, see "blend modes" in the PhotoPlus Help's index.

A tool or layer's **Opacity** setting interacts with its blend mode to produce varying results. For details, see Adjusting opacity/transparency on p. 150.

To set a tool's blend mode:

- Select the tool and use the drop-down list (displays Normal by default) on the tool's Context toolbar.

To set a standard layer's blend mode:

- Select the layer and choose the mode from the **Blend Mode** drop-down list.

Using blend ranges

A Blend Mode can be associated with a tool or layer to produce different colour effects when pixels from each layer are painted on top of each other. **Blend ranges**, a more advanced blending feature, differ in that they specify the range of colours on a current layer that is to be blended with the underlying layer—this is a simple include or exclude of tones or colours in the blending process.

Just like blend modes, blend ranges are created and modified in the **Layer Properties** dialog.

The blend range can be set for Red, Green, Blue or Grey channels. The upper layer (**This Layer**) and its **Underlying Layer** can each be allocated a value from 0\0 to 255\255 each which represents the tonal or colour value—value pairs (e.g., 70\70 or 255\255) are set by moving the triangular sliders to the required value on the range selector. In the example above, the grey tones of value less than 70 are not included in the blend. This means that the colour of the underlying layers pixels is used instead (as there is no blending taking place).

To apply a blend range:

1. Open an image that possesses more than one layer.

2. Go to the Layers tab. Decide which two layers you want to apply a blend range between.

3. Double-click the upper layer.

4. In the Blend Ranges box, specify a channel to work on in the **Channel** drop-down menu – choose Grey, Red, Green or Blue.

5. On the **This Layer** range selector, drag either the lower or upper sliders right or left, respectively, to limit the blend range. You can drag both sliders to reduce both the upper and lower ranges if you wish.

6. Do the same for the **Underlying Layer**.

7. Click **OK** to apply the blend range.

With the **Alt** key, smoothing is possible by splitting the triangular sliders into two and moving one half to a new position on the range selector. The greater the difference in values, the greater the smoothing applied.

Adjusting opacity/transparency

Opacity and **transparency** describe essentially the same thing (like "half full" and "half empty"). They both describe the degree to which a particular pixel's colour contributes to the overall colour at that point in the image.

Varying opacity is rather like lighting a gauze backdrop in a theatre: depending on how light falls on it, it can be rendered either visible or invisible, or in between. Fully opaque pixels contribute their full colour value to the image. Fully transparent pixels are invisible: they contribute nothing to the image. In-between pixels are called semi-transparent. You'll primarily encounter opacity in one of these two contexts:

- As a property of the pixels laid down by individual **tools** (Paintbrush, Clone, Eraser, Fill, Smudge, QuickShape, and more) . When you paint on-screen with one of these tools, you're applying pixels—pixels that are more or less opaque, depending on the tool's opacity setting. Note that once you've applied paint to a region, that's it—you've changed the opacity of pixels there. Subsequently changing a tool's opacity setting won't alter brush strokes you've already laid down!

- As a property of individual **standard layers** (as in the example above). The layer's opacity setting affects all the pixels on the layer, and is cumulative with the opacity of individual pixels already there.

  A tool or layer's **blend mode** interacts with its opacity setting to produce varying results. For details, see Using blend modes on p. 147.

To set a tool's opacity:

- Select the tool (e.g., Paintbrush Tool) and from the Context toolbar either enter a percentage **Opacity** value directly or use the slider (click the option's right arrow button).

To set a layer's opacity:

- Select the layer in the Layers tab and adjust the **Opacity** setting at the top of the tab—either enter a percentage **Opacity** value directly or use the slider (click the option's right button). The layer's opacity will change on-screen as the slider is adjusted.

To read the opacity values of pixels on the active layer:

1. Select the ✐ **Colour Pickup Tool** from the **Tools** toolbar and move it around the image.

2. Read the value shown for "O" (Opacity) on the HintLine (e.g., O:80%).
   The readout updates constantly, showing the opacity value of each
   pixel under the cursor.

For more useful hints and tips about using opacity, see PhotoPlus help.

Using depth maps

Depth maps let you add remarkable 3D realism to ordinary images. A standard
"flat" image, of course, has only two dimensions: X and Y, or width and height.
Adding a depth map to a layer gives you an extra channel that stores
information for a third (Z-axis or depth) dimension, in effect adding "volume" to
the image. It's as if the original image acquires a surface with peaks and valleys—
and you can play with the elevation of the landscape to achieve different visual
results.

The example opposite was created simply by painting
in white (on a green background) with a fuzzy brush
on the depth map.

Changes on the "map" layer produce the effect of
highs and lows in the "surface"... it's like using a 3D
brush!

You can also combine depth maps with pre-defined 3D effects hosted in the
Instant Effects tab to create fascinating surfaces and textures—simply click on a
thumbnail from one of the tab's categorized galleries with your layer containing
the depth map selected, e.g.

Elements -
Fire Storm

Abstract -
Plasma

Stone -
Polished Stone

To create a depth map:

1. Select the layer (or group) in the Layers tab and click 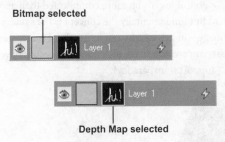 **Add Layer Depth Map**.

   You'll see a thumbnail of the depth map appear to the right of the bitmap thumbnail. The Depth Map is initially selected.

   Bitmap selected

   Depth Map selected

2. Paint directly on your page (you're actually painting or erasing directly on the map). Your brush stroke on the depth map produces interesting depressions and ridges on the image, which are exposed by 3D lighting effects automatically applied from the 3D Effects category.

While working on the layer, you can switch back and forth between the bitmap, depth map, and (optional) mask by clicking the appropriate layer thumbnail. You can also switch the depth map off and on to assess its contribution to the image, or subtract it for creative reasons.

To switch the depth map off and on:

- **Shift**-click its preview thumbnail, next to the layer name. When the depth map is switched off a red 'X' appears across the thumbnail.

To remove the depth map and cancel its effects on the layer:

- Select the map thumbnail and click the layer tab's 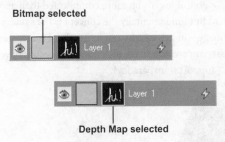 **Delete** button. (Don't press the **Delete** key!)

Importing a depth map

Another way of incorporating a depth map is to create a suitable bitmap image separately (or borrow one from somewhere else) and then paste it via the Clipboard to an existing PhotoPlus depth map.

Using masks

Masking in a program like PhotoPlus is a bit more complicated than applying masking tape to the screen! But fundamentally the concept is the same: you can hide certain parts of an image—in this case by rendering them transparent, hence invisible. To do that, you create a **mask** on a non-Background layer (the Background layer doesn't support transparency).

By changing the **greyscale** values on the mask (using the paint tools and other devices), you can impose corresponding changes in the **opacity** of the underlying layer's pixels (values stored as the layer's **alpha channel**) . For example, by applying a gradient "blacking out" across the mask, you gradually render the layer's underlying pixels transparent, and they disappear from the image (see above).

Besides the creative possibilities, ranging from vignetting to multi-layer montage to gradient-fill masking (see example above) and beyond, a great feature of working on a mask is that it is "temporary." If you don't like the way things are going, you can abandon your changes and start over without ever having affected the actual pixels on the layer!

Each non-Background layer can have one mask at any given time. (The Background layer can't have one because it doesn't support transparency.) Mask information, like layer information, can only be preserved by saving the image in the native PhotoPlus (.SPP) format.

Creating the mask

Before you can use a mask, you have to create it on a particular layer. The mask can start out as transparent (revealing the whole layer), opaque (hiding the whole layer), a transparency gradient (opposite) or—if you create it from a selection—a bit of both (with only the selected region hidden or revealed). The mask shows as a mask thumbnail.

The choice depends on how you want to work with the layer's contents. By darkening portions of a clear mask, you can selectively fade underlying layer pixels. By lightening an opaque mask, you selectively reveal layer pixels.

To create a mask:

1. Select a layer in the Layers tab. This is the layer where you want to create the mask, and select specific region(s) if desired.

2. Then either:

   - Click the [icon] **Add Layer Mask** button to create a Reveal All mask (or Reveal Selection if there is one). Instead, **Alt**-click the button for a Hide All Mask (or Hide Selection).
   OR

   - Choose **Mask>Add Mask** from the **Layers** menu and then one of the following from the submenu:

- **Reveal All** for a transparent mask over the whole layer
- **Hide All** for an opaque mask over the whole layer
- **Reveal Selection** for an opaque mask with transparent "holes" over the selected region(s)
- **Hide Selection** for a transparent mask with opaque "blocks" over the selected region(s)

On the Layers tab, a mask preview thumbnail appears, confirming that a mask exists.

Editing on the mask

When you create your mask you immediately enter Edit Mask mode, where you can use the full range of painting tools, selection options, flood fills, gradient fills, and effects to alter the mask's greyscale values. These manipulations cause corresponding changes in opacity, which in turn changes the appearance of the pixels on the layer itself.

The image window's titlebar shows "[MASK]," indicating that a mask is currently being edited. The Colour tab switches to Greyscale mode when you're editing a mask, and reverts to the previous setting when you exit Edit Mask mode. This means anything you paste from the Clipboard onto the mask will automatically be converted to greyscale.

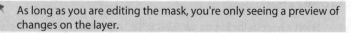 As long as you are editing the mask, you're only seeing a preview of changes on the layer.

You can switch out of Edit Mask mode at any time to edit the active layer directly (or any other part of the image), then switch back to resume work on the mask.

To edit the active layer:

- Click the layer thumbnail to the left of the Mask thumbnail. The thumbnail is then bordered in white.

To edit the active layer's mask:

- Click the mask thumbnail, or check **Edit Mask** on the **Layers** menu.

In Edit Mask mode, you're normally viewing not the mask, but rather the effects of changes "as if" you were making them on the layer below. Adding a Reveal All mask can be a bit confusing, because there's initially no evidence the mask is there at all (i.e. the layer appears exactly the same as it did before you added the mask)!

It's sometimes helpful to switch on the **View Mask** setting, which hides the layer and lets you see **only** the mask, in all its greyscale glory. For example, a Reveal All mask appears pure white in View Mask mode—the white represents a clear mask with no effect on the underlying layer pixels' opacity. View Mask can also be useful in the latter stages of working on a mask, to locate any small regions that may have escaped your attention.

To view the active layer's mask:

- **Alt**-click the mask preview thumbnail. **Alt**-click again to stop viewing the mask.

White or light portions of the mask reveal layer pixels (make them more opaque). Black or dark portions hide layer pixels (making them more transparent).

You can **disable** the mask to see how the layer looks without the mask's effects. Note that disabling the mask is not the same as cancelling Edit Mask mode—it only affects your view of the layer, not which plane (i.e. mask or layer) you're working on.

To disable the active layer's mask:

 Shift-click the mask preview thumbnail, or check **Disable Mask** on the Layers menu. (**Shift**-click again or uncheck the menu item to enable masking again.)
When the mask is disabled, a red "X" appears across its thumbnail.

If you want to fine-tune a mask or layer's position independently of each other it's possible to **unlink** them. You may have noticed a small link button between the layer and mask thumbnails on the Layers tab, i.e.

A click on this button will unlink the layer and mask, changing the button to display a red cross through it ( ). By selecting the layer or mask thumbnail, you can then drag the layer or mask on the page, respectively. After fine-tuning, click the button to relink the mask to the layer.

Masks and selections

Suffice it to say that a selection, which lets you isolate specific parts of the active layer, often makes an ideal basis for a mask. Once you've created, modified, and manipulated a selection, it's easy to turn it into a mask.

To create a mask from a selection:

1. Choose **Mask>Add Mask** from the **Layers** menu. Remember you can't create a mask on a background layer!

2. To create a mask revealing the selected region, choose **Reveal Selection** from the submenu. Pixels outside the selection will be 100% masked.
   OR
   To create a mask hiding the selected region, choose **Hide Selection** from the submenu. Pixels outside the selection will be revealed.

You can also select part of an image to create a custom brush shape, for example a textured brush or special shape.

Conversely, you can **create a selection** directly from the mask by **Ctrl**-clicking on the layer's mask thumbnail. Within the resulting selection, pixels that are lighter on the mask (conferring more opacity) become relatively more selected. This correlates with Paint to Select mode (see p. 42), where painting in lighter tones also confers "selectedness."

7

Creating Animations

Getting started with animation

Animation creates an illusion of motion or change by displaying a series of still pictures, rapidly enough to fool the eye—or more accurately, the brain. With PhotoPlus, it's easy to create and edit images with multiple frames, then export them as **animated GIFs** that a Web browser can play back, or **AVI movies** for multimedia applications. You use exactly the same tools and interface as for creating standard, multi-layer PhotoPlus images, with an extra tab, the Animation tab, that includes all the additional controls you need to set up frames, add special effects, and preview the animation. Once you're satisfied, use the Export Optimizer to output to Animated GIF or AVI movie.

PhotoPlus gives you the choice of creating your animations from scratch, importing a .GIF or .AVI file to edit, or converting existing photos to an animation by selecting **Convert to Animation** from the **File** menu. Either way, once PhotoPlus detects an animation file, it switches on the Animation tab. If the image file is new, you'll see a single, blank frame, labelled "Frame 1." If you've imported an animation, the tab displays each frame separately. Animation files can have one layer, or many (see below), but all their layers are standard (transparent) layers; there's no Background layer. If a photo is used, the first frame will be the photo image.

> The Animation tab only displays when an animation is currently open.

Layers and frames

Animations are created in the **Animation tab** (docked next to the Documents tab at the bottom of your workspace) which works in conjunction with the **Layers tab**. The tab displays a sequence of frame thumbnails. Each frame is a different state of the image, defined in terms of which layers are shown or hidden, the position of content on each shown layer, and the opacity of each shown layer.

In this file (as in any imported .GIF animation) the individual frames can each occupy one layer in the PhotoPlus image. This is controlled with the **Add Layer to Each New Frame** check box, available by right-clicking the Animation tab. Each new frame can therefore be edited independently as it occupies its own layer.

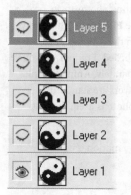

On the Layers tab, the layer stack for this animation corresponds with the frame sequence, with default names—in this case, the default "Layer 1" through to "Layer 5". You'll notice the thumbnails correlate between frame and layer.

If you select Frame 1 on the Animation tab (above), you'll see that on the Layers tab (left) only the "Layer 1" layer is marked as shown, with an open-eye button; the other layers are all hidden, with closed-eye buttons.

If you then select Frame 2, only the "Layer 2" layer will be shown, and the rest will be hidden. And so on with the other frames.

The above example, with its one-to-one correspondence between frames and layers, is easy to grasp—but don't make the mistake of thinking that a "frame" is just another name for a "layer." Frames in PhotoPlus are actually much more versatile!

Key point: A so-called "frame" is really just a particular state or snapshot of the various layers in the image, in terms of three layer properties:

- **Shown/Hidden:** Which layers are shown and which are hidden

- **Position:** The position of the contents of each "shown" layer

- **Opacity:** The opacity setting of each "shown" layer

As you switch between frames, you switch between states. In the simple example above, the six frames define six states in terms of Property 1—each of the six frames defines a different layer as "shown." We could rearrange the stacking order of the layers, or rename them—the animation itself wouldn't change.

When you create a new frame on the Animation tab, you're not adding a new layer. The new frame merely enables you to define a new state of the layers that already exist. Of course, you could go on and create an additional layer (using the Layers tab), but then all your animation frames would need to take that layer into account—in other words, hide it when it wasn't needed.

Single-layer animation

Let's look at a different example (below) which shows the Yin-Yang symbol as a bouncing ball, and although it has four frames it only has one layer (Add Layer to Each New Frame was unchecked). Three additional frames were cloned from Frame 1 (using the **New Frame** button), and then, within each subsequent frame the layer was dragged slightly (with the Move Tool) to reposition its contents in the window.

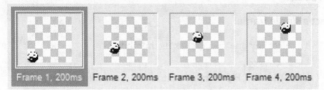

Frame 1, 200ms   Frame 2, 200ms   Frame 3, 200ms   Frame 4, 200ms

Working with animation frames

Let's cover the "nuts and bolts" of creating and arranging animation frames using the Animation tab. You'll use the tab in conjunction with the Layers tab to varying extents, but we'll focus on the Animation tab for the moment.

Here are some general guidelines to help you produce memorable animations:

1. Decide if you want layers to be created with each frame. Check or uncheck the **Add Layer to Each New Frame** option (if needed) by right-clicking on the Animation tab. This means that each new frame can be edited independently as it occupies its own layer.

2. Create enough frames to define the separate states of the animation.

3. Step through the frames, adjusting layer content and state for each frame. You can delete or reposition frames as needed, and preview the animation at any time.

4. Save the animation as a regular PhotoPlus (.SPP) file, and export it to the .GIF or .AVI format.

To create a new frame:

*   Click the ▦ **New Frame** button (or right-click a thumbnail and choose **New Frame**).

The previously selected frame is cloned as a new frame, immediately following it in the sequence.

To select a single frame:

*   To select any one frame, click its thumbnail.

*   Click the ◁ **First Frame** button to select the first frame of the sequence (rewind).

*   Click the ◁▯ **Previous Frame** button to select the previous frame of the sequence.
    If the first frame was selected, you'll cycle back to the last frame of the sequence.

- Click the **Next Frame** button to select the next frame of the sequence.
  If the last frame of the sequence was selected, you'll cycle forward to the first frame.

- Click the **Last Frame** button to select the last frame of the sequence.

To select more than one frame:

- To select multiple non-adjacent frames, hold down the **Ctrl** key when selecting each one.

- To select a range of adjacent frames, hold down the **Shift** key and click the first and last thumbnail in the range.

To speed up the animation process:

- **Tweening**, short for "in-betweening", automatically creates a chosen number of frames between the currently selected frame and the previous or next frame. This gives a smoother transition of your animation during playback and saves you time.
  • Set the number of new frames to be created between the next and previous frames.
  • Apply the tweening to just the currently selected layer or all layers.
  • Set which frame attributes are to be tweened—choose Position, Opacity and/or Effects. Position lets you distribute frame objects evenly between next and previous frames (great for creating motion quickly).

- To clone multiple frames, select (see above) then click the **New Frame** button. To clone all frames, right-click the tab and choose **Select All** then clone.

- Use **Reverse Frames** on the right-click menu to reverse the order of a series of selected frames. For example, for bouncing ball animations, create the animated ball as if it were being dropped, use the above "clone all frame" technique on all frames, then reverse the newly cloned frames while selected. You may need to remove the first of the cloned frames because of duplication.

To mirror a frame layer's attributes:

- To mirror the attributes of a frames' layers with respect to Position, Opacity, Blend Mode, Visibility and Effects, select specific or all frames (see above) ensuring that the "target" frame which possesses the attribute(s) to be copied is selected **first**, then choose **Unify Layer Across Frames**. All "destination" frames adopt the layer attributes of the "target" frame.

To delete one or more frames:

- Select the thumbnail(s) and click the 🗑 **Delete Frame** button. (To delete a single frame, you can also right-click it and choose **Delete**.)

To reposition a frame in the sequence:

- Drag its thumbnail and drop it before or after another frame. Note the black vertical insertion cursor to indicate the proposed new position of a frame.

To play (preview) the animation:

- Click the ▷ **Play** button.

The Animation tab includes two options—one global, the other local—that you should consider before exporting the animation.

- For .GIFs (not .AVIs), you can set a **loop** property for the animation as a whole. (You can also set this property on the Animation tab of the Export Optimizer.)

  ⇥| If you want the sequence to play through only once and end displaying the first frame, click the **Fixed Loop** button and enter "1" in the box. Enter a higher value to repeat the sequence a fixed number of times.

  Click the 🔁 **Endless Loop** button to have the sequence repeat indefinitely.

- If the playback of certain frames (or all frames) seems too fast, you can select any frame and enter a value greater than 0 in the **Frame Delay** field. The frame's delay factor (in milliseconds) will be exported along with the .GIF. Sometimes all frames may require a delay factor in order to achieve proper pacing. You can select multiple (or all) frames and enter a common value in the Frame Delay field.

To stop the animation:

- Click the 🔲 **Stop** button.

To export the animation as a .GIF file:

- Choose **Export Optimizer...** from the **File** menu. The animated GIF format is selected as default.

For details on exporting, see Exporting to another file format on p. 199.

To preview the animation in your Web browser:

- Choose **Preview in Browser** from the **File** menu. PhotoPlus exports the image as a temporary file, then opens the file for preview in your Web browser.

To flatten your frames:

- For more complex animations, your animation project can be simplified by flattening all frames (individual frames cannot be flattened); right-click and choose **Flatten Frames**. Multiple layers associated with frames are replaced by a single layer; layer objects are no longer independent and are therefore no longer editable.

Applying animation effects

You can turn a variety of PhotoPlus effects (those found on the **Effects** menu) into animated transition sequences. The process "in-betweens" or "morphs" a layer from a designated starting frame into an end state over a specified number of frames, creating one new layer per frame. You have the option of creating brand new frames or spreading the sequence over existing frames. If you like, you can select a "Ping Pong" option that builds in a reverse sequence so the end state visually matches the starting point.

You can either have PhotoPlus create a sequence of new frames for the effect (check **Create as new frames**) or you can create some empty frames yourself and then generate the effect with the **Create as new frames** option unchecked. This will integrate the new layers into the existing blank frames, beginning with the designated Start frame.

> ✦ To use text or shapes with animation effects, first merge the text or shape layer into a standard layer, or convert it to a standard layer by right-clicking on the layer name and choosing Rasterize from the flyout menu.

To apply a special effect:

1. Select the frame, and the specific layer on the frame, you want to use as the starting point (we'll just call this the "Start frame").

2. Click the ⚡ **Effects** button on the Animation tab to display the Animation Effects dialog. The dialog provides two preview windows (for the Start and End frames) that initially display the contents of the selected layer.

3. Click an effect name in the Effects list. The dialog changes to provide custom controls for each effect (try clicking on different effects for a preview).

4. Click the left-hand (Start Preview) window to set properties for the starting frame (note the red border when selected), adjust the controls or enter values, then click the right-hand (End Preview) window and choose settings for the final frame, as the preview windows update.

5. To set the length of the sequence, enter a value in the **Number of Frames** box. The process will create a series of new "shown" layers, with one new layer per frame. In other words, a six-frame sequence always adds six new layers to the image.

6. Check **Create as new frames** if you want to put the sequence into a series of new frames, beginning immediately after the designated Start frame. If you uncheck this option, the new layers will be integrated into existing frames (which should be blank if you want to see the results!), beginning with the Start frame.

7. To set a delay factor (to be applied to each frame in the sequence), enter a value in the **Frame Delay** box.

8. Check **Ping Pong** to build a "two-way" sequence that morphs to the end state and back again. This works for .GIFs, but not .AVIs. (If you choose this option, remember to increase the number of frames or cut the frame delay to maintain visual pacing.)

9. To preview the animation, click the ▷ **Play** and ☐ **Stop** buttons. The sequence appears in the End preview window. (Note that because the effect filter must work "on the fly," timing in preview mode may not be accurate.)

10. Click **OK** to apply the effect, or **Cancel** to abandon changes.

8

Making Images for the web

Slicing images

Image slicing and **image maps** are two convenient ways to create navbars (navigation bars) and clickable graphics for Web pages. With image slicing, a graphic is carved up into smaller graphics—each of which can have its own link, like any Web graphic—and PhotoPlus saves the sections as separate files when you export the image. The process also exports HTML tags describing a table containing the separate graphics, allowing a Web browser to reassemble them seamlessly. The result appears as a single larger graphic, but with different regions linked to different targets.

For example, the menubar graphic (below top)... can be sliced into four separate graphics (below bottom), each linked to a different Web page.

The Image Slice Tool lets you divide the image into sections which can be exported to the .GIF or .JPG file format. You can specify alternate text and URL links for each of the image sections individually.

To slice the image:

- Choose the ![icon] **Image Slice Tool** from the **Standard** toolbar.

- To place a horizontal slice guide on the image, click on the image at your chosen cursor position. **Shift**-click to place a vertical guide. A red guide line appears with each click.

- To move a guide, simply drag it.

- To delete a guide, drag it out of the image window.

To specify the alternate text and/or link:

- Right-click an image slice (any area enclosed by horizontal and vertical slice guides) and enter the alternate **Text** and **URL** (link) information in the dialog.

Once you've sliced up your image you have to export it to make the image slices understandable to a Web visitor's browser.

To export a sliced image:

- When exporting with **File>Export Optimizer**, ensure the **Create Image Slices** box is checked on the second Export dialog. Specify a name and folder for the files as usual, and choose either .GIF or .JPG as the export file type.

  Since exporting slices creates multiple files, you may wish to create a separate folder for them.

The export will create multiple files in the specified folder, depending on how many slices you have defined. The output consists of a series of image files of the format selected (for example, MYFILEH0V0.GIF, MYFILEH0V1.GIF, etc.) and a single HTML file (for example, MYFILE.HTM). The HTML file contains the tags for the set of image slices, ready to be pasted into the source code for the Web page.

Creating image maps

Whereas image slicing subdivides an entire graphic into smaller graphics and exports them separately, image maps consist of **hotspots** that you draw with special tools over selected parts of an image. When a visitor passes their mouse cursor over the hotspot, a small caption is displayed and the pointer will change to a pointing hand. Clicking the mouse while the cursor is over the hotspot will invoke a hyperlink to a specified URL.

You assign each hotspot its own target—for example, the URL of a Web page. Hotspots aren't attached to a particular image, but become part of a larger "map" that gets exported along with an image and turns into HTML code. It's then up to the Web developer to embed the image map code properly into the Web page.

The **Image Map Tools** flyout on the **Standard** toolbar displays a flyout menu of tools for creating and editing image maps.

Image maps are useful if you want to define isolated and/or irregularly shaped clickable regions on a Web graphic, as opposed to subdividing the entire graphic into rectangular image slices.

To draw a hotspot:

1. Click the **Image Map Tools** flyout on the **Standard** toolbar and choose one of the following tools:

   ☐ **Image Map Rectangle**

   ○ **Image Map Circle**

   ◺ **Image Map Polygon**

2. For rectangles and circles, use the tool to drag out a hotspot on the active layer. To draw a polygon, drag and release the mouse button to define each line segment; double-click to close the polygon. All hotspots are shaded in turquoise.

   When using the Image Map Rectangle, hold down the Ctrl key while dragging out to constrain the hotspot's shape to a square.

To edit a hotspot:

1.   Click the **Image Map Tools** flyout and choose the **Image Map Selection** tool.

2.   To resize the hotspot, drag from an edge.

3.   To move the hotspot, drag from the centre.

4.   Right-click the hotspot to set hotspot **Properties....** Enter hover-over **Text** and add an associated target **URL**. Previously used URLs are saved and can be selected from the drop-down list by clicking on the arrow at the end of the box. On export, entered text will pop up when the cursor moves over the hotspot.

5.   (Optional) The right-click menu also lets you order overlapping hotspots and to **Delete** selected hotspots.

To export an image map:

●   When exporting via Export Optimizer, check the **Create HTML for Image Maps** box on the second Export dialog.

The output consists of an image file and an HTML file with the same base name. The HTML file contains the tags for the image map, ready to be pasted into the source code for the Web page.

9
Macros and Batch Processing

Understanding macros

If there are operations that you want to repeatedly perform in PhotoPlus, you can apply a **macro**. Put simply, a macro is a saved sequence of commands that can be stored and then recalled at a later date. Macros can be used for:

- Downsampling

- Reformatting

- Applying effects

- Image adjustments

There are hundreds, possibly thousands, of macros that could be recorded for PhotoPlus. The good news is that PhotoPlus already offers a wide range of pre-recorded macros ready for your use. These macros are available in the Macros tab, where they are separated into various categories including Black & White Photography, Colour, Commands, Vignettes, Layout Blurs, and Frames (shown) to name but a few.

You'll notice an  icon next to each macro which, when clicked, displays the commands that make up the macro (click to collapse again). For example, a macro that creates a wood frame would have a series of recorded commands listed chronologically. They may be enabled, disabled, reordered or made interactive "on the fly".

You can cut, copy, paste or even duplicate any macro. This allows you to modify pre-defined macros once pasted into your own user-defined categories.

Recording Macros

Of course at some point you may want to record your own macro. It's probably a good idea to create a new category into which you can save your newly recorded macros—this keeps them separate from the pre-recorded macros supplied with PhotoPlus. This is because recorded macros will be indistinguishable from your preset macros once recorded.

When recording macros, it can be a good idea to ensure that the Layout Rulers/Grid units in **File>Preferences** are set to "percent". This approach ensures that recorded macro commands such as document resizing or framing are carried out in proportion to the original photo rather than by an absolute value. Imagine adding an absolute frame size to a small photo that would otherwise be acceptable on the larger photo. On some occasions you may want to use absolute values—simply use absolute grid units.

> Try to plan ahead before recording—If you jot down your intended command sequence you'll make fewer mistakes!

To create a new category:

1.   Display the **Macros** tab.

2.   Click the ⬚ **New Category** button at the bottom of the Macros tab.

3.   In the dialog, enter a new category name and click **OK**. The new empty category is displayed automatically.

> Any currently displayed category can be edited or deleted via the ▷ Tab Menu button at the top right of the Macros tab.

To record a macro:

1.   In the Macros tab, select a category from the drop-down list of category names.

2.   Click the ⬚ **New Macro** button at the bottom of the Macros tab to provide a macro name in advance of recording your macro. The

macro name appears at the bottom of the list of macros in the currently displayed category.

3. Select the ⭕ **Start Recording** button. Any command that can be saved in a macro will be stored while recording is in progress.

4. Carry out the command sequence you want to record, following the instructions when necessary.

5. Stop recording your macro with the ▢ **Stop Recording** button!

To view the macro, navigate to the correct category, then click on the ▷ icon to expand the entry to show the command list recorded by the macro.

Playing Macros

To play a macro you need to choose a photo to which you want to apply your recorded or pre-recorded macro. Any macro needs to be played to repeat the recorded commands.

To play a macro:

1. Open the photo you wish to apply the macro to.

2. From the **Macros** tab, choose a category from the drop-down menu, then select your macro.

3. Choose the ▷ **Play** button in the Macros tab to play the macro.

🔖 Abort any macro playback at any time with the ESC key.

Modifying Macros

Once you've recorded and played back your macro it's possible to modify the macro's saved sequence of commands. These are listed in the order they were recorded and may be enabled, disabled, reordered or made interactive "on the fly". Macro commands are enabled by default.

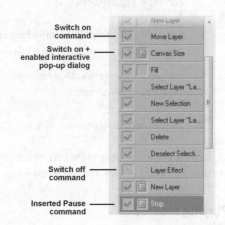

Switch on command

Switch on + enabled interactive pop-up dialog

Switch off command

Inserted Pause command

It is also possible to perform a right-click to delete, rename or duplicate a command from the flyout menu. In the command list, the command order can be rearranged by simple drag and drop of any command into a new position.

Any changes made will be applied to the macro immediately such that no file saving is required.

★ It is possible to copy and paste pre-defined macros to any user-defined category but not individual commands within each macro.

★ Warning: If you significantly modify your macro command list your macro may become unusable, so it's important to exercise some restraint while editing—experimentation and testing is the rule of thumb.

To switch a command off:

1. Go to the **Macros** tab.

2. Choose a category from the drop-down menu.

3. Decide which macro you want to modify.

4. Click the ▷ icon next to the macro name to reveal the macro's command list in the drop-down menu.

5. Each list entry begins with a check box ✓ which switches on or off the relevant command. Uncheck the box to switch the command off.

> 🔖 Experimentation is required when switching commands on or off—some commands are integral to the way a macro operates!

To enable command interactivity:

This allows you to intervene in the macro running process to alter some dialog values, i.e. the next time a macro is played, the macro will pop-up the relevant dialog associated with a command, pausing the macro temporarily. For example, for a "Frames" macro, the **Canvas Size** dialog could be made to display during macro playback to allow new canvas dimensions to be entered manually (try some pre-defined Frames macros + options for examples of this).

1. Go to the **Macros** tab.

2. Choose a category from the drop-down menu.

3. Decide on a macro which is to be made interactive.

4. Click the ▷ icon next to the chosen macro's name to reveal the macro's command list in the drop-down menu.

5. Click the empty box before a command name to display the 🗐 **Enable\Disable Dialog** icon.

6. Load a photo and play the modified macro. The macro pauses to display a dialog associated with the above command name.

7. Modify any settings and press the **OK** button. The macro will continue.

To switch off command interactivity, simply click the icon again.

> ★ Did you spot that some commands have no "interactive" boxes?
> This is because some commands by their nature have no dialogs
> associated with them!

To add manual instructions to your command list:

Another example of interactivity is the inclusion of a pause into your macro.
This allows you to pop up manual instructions (or important notes) in a dialog
at pre-defined points as your macro runs. There are a number of reasons for
doing this—your macro can't record selections or operations that are particular
to each photo so manual selection is essential in some instances, or maybe you
want to add a helpful note (e.g., "perform a brush stroke") or warning in advance
of a required action or dialog.

1. Right-click on a command in a macro's command list and select **Insert
    Pause...** from the flyout menu.

2. Add some relevant notes into the **Stop Options** dialog—check **Allow
    continue** if you want to present a **Continue** button in your dialog as
    the macro runs. Clicking the button will continue the macro process.

3. Click **OK**. The **Stop** command is added to the command list below the
    command you performed a right-click on (you may want to drag it to
    before the command).

4. Load a photo and play the modified macro (see **Playing Macros**
    above). The macro pauses to display a dialog with your instructions—
    remember these before the next step!

5. Click the **Stop** button.

6. Perform the task(s) as instructed in the dialog.

7. Press the button to continue the macro from the next command
    in the list after the **Stop** command.

> ★ If you don't need to perform the manual operation, click Continue
> to continue the macro without pausing.

Copying, duplicating and deleting Macros

With the vast collection of macros and commands at your disposal, it's useful to know that you can copy preset or user-defined macros to any user-defined category for modification—simply right-click on the macro to be copied and select **Copy**. You can paste the macro by right-click then selecting **Paste** (the macro will be added to the end of the category list). Additionally, commands can be moved (as opposed to copied) between any user-defined macros by drag and drop.

> ★ You can't copy macros or commands into any pre-defined category.

User-defined macros and their associated commands can also be duplicated (or deleted) by right-click and selection of the **Duplicate** (or **Delete**) command.

Batch processing

The batch processing feature is especially useful if you want to repeat the same operation again and again... Batch processing allows you to:

- Use Macro: uses pre-recorded or user-defined macros as part of the batch process.

- Change File Type: to bulk convert images to a new file type (with different file properties if needed).

- Resize Images: to resample images to various widths, heights, or resolutions (using different resampling methods).

- Change File Name: to alter the file names of images in bulk.

For any of the above, you specify separate source and destination folders as your input and output. There are several advantages to this, mainly that your original photos are not overwritten.

The **Batch** dialog, available from the **File** menu, is used to perform all of the above operations.

As a pre-requisite, you have to define a specific **Source Folder** for any batch processing operation, whether using a macro or not, or if converting photos to a different file format.

A **Destination folder** can optionally be defined, creating new files in that new location (otherwise the source folder is used, overwriting original images).

To save you time, PhotoPlus will remember previously selected Source and Destination folders while PhotoPlus is loaded.

You may be wondering how batch processing affects photos currently loaded in PhotoPlus. PhotoPlus's batch processing only operates on source folder contents and not on the currently loaded photos themselves—so these remain unaffected. However, as a visual check, you will see each photo temporarily being loaded and converted one-by-one in the Photo window during batch processing.

> Check the output folder via Windows Explorer to ensure the results are as you expect.

Using macros

Macros (see p. 179) can be applied to a batch process easily. Click the **Use Macro** check box and pick a category and macro name. PhotoPlus doesn't differentiate between pre-recorded and recorded macros. If available, they are selected from the same **Category** and **Macro** drop-down menus equally.

Changing file type

It is possible to convert your photos into one of many different file types available in PhotoPlus. In addition, conversion options such as bit depth, palette, dithering, compression/quality, and matte can be selected depending on the file type.

Changing image size

As well as changing file formats, PhotoPlus can use batch processing to alter image sizes in bulk (using a choice of resampling methods). Typically, this is a quick and easy way to make your images scale to a maximum image dimension (height or width) with aspect ratio maintained, to absolute image dimensions (with stretching/shrinking to fit), scale by percentage, and scale by resolution (DPI). Use for sending your digital photos via email or perhaps to publish your images online via a web site.

Check **Maintain aspect ratio** then enter values for **Max Width** and **Max Height** to scale to maximum intended dimensions while preserving the image's original aspect ratio.

With **Maintain aspect ratio** unchecked, enter values for absolute **Width** and **Height** to make images of a fixed size. As aspect ratio is not maintained, images may be stretched horizontally or vertically.

Change the units of measurement to percent, then enter identical percentage values to scale **Width** and **Height** in proportion (maintain aspect ratio); otherwise, different values will stretch images horizontally or vertically.

Resolution: 96 dpi

Enter a DPI value to alter the original resolution of the images.

Resampling Method:

Pick a method from the drop-down list. Use Nearest Pixel for hard-edge images, Bilinear Interpolation when shrinking photos, Bicubic Interpolation when enlarging photos, and Lanczos3 Window when best quality results are expected. The list is ordered according to processing times (fastest to slowest).

Changing file names

It is also possible to define a Destination **File Name** for the files to be processed by selecting the dialog's **Modify...** button. In the **File Name Format** dialog you can select new file names that can be built up using the current date/time, document names, sequence number, or text string, individually or in combination. Remember to use the sequence number to generate a separate file for every file to be converted—otherwise your first converted file will be overwritten continually.

10
Printing and Exporting

10

Printing and
Exporting

Printing

For basic printing primarily to desktop printers, PhotoPlus offers an exciting, comprehensive, and versatile printing solution for your photos.

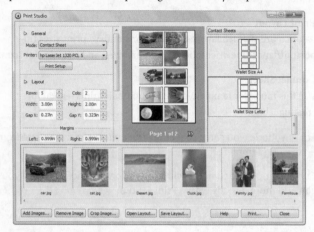

The easy-to-use **Print Studio** lets you easily jump between different **print modes**, each mode designed for **single-** or **multi-image** printing of differing print layouts. Multi-image printing in PhotoPlus lets you make the most of expensive photo quality printing paper by "ganging" several images onto a single output sheet using a **print layout** or **contact sheet** template (shown above).

- **Single Image**
  Use for basic desktop printing of an individual image, with supporting Layout options (image scaling, positioning, and tiling) and template choices.

- **Print Layout**
  Adopt a pre-defined layout template for standard print sizes (in portrait/landscape orientation), passport sizes, and mixed print sizes.

- **Contact Sheet**
  Use this mode for template-driven thumbnail prints—great for creating labels!

For any mode, you can also create your own custom template from an existing template.

Currently open documents will be used for printing, although you can add more directly within Print Studio.

To print:

1. Click the 🖶 **Print** button on the **Standard** toolbar.

   The Print Studio appears which shows your currently open images as thumbnails in a scrolling gallery at the bottom of your workspace, a page layout region in the centre, a selection of templates at the right, and a print mode/options pane to the left.

2. From the **Mode** drop-down menu, select a mode from **Single Image, Print Layout**, or **Contact Sheets**.

3. Choose a **Printer** from the drop-down menu. Click Print Setup... to set up the printer for the correct page size, portrait (tall), or landscape (wide) orientation. The preview window may change according to your printer setup.

4. From the right-hand template list, select a template specific to the mode selected.

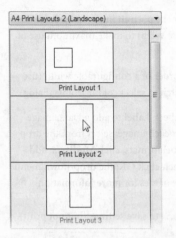

- Choose a category which matches your current print mode, e.g. in Print Layout mode, pick a Print Layout category.

- To insert a particular template into the central page layout region, simply click its gallery thumbnail.

> A print layout's cells need to be manually populated; other modes will auto-populate cells.

5. Depending on print mode, decide on which images are to be used for printing, i.e.

- To replace an image in **Single Image mode**, you can select a different image from the lower image gallery.

- To populate your layout in **Print Layout mode**, right-click a gallery thumbnail and select **Fill Layout with Image**. All occupied or empty cells in your layout are replaced. Alternatively, to fill an individual cell, drag a replacement image from the lower image gallery onto the "target" cell. A print layout's cells need to be manually populated; other modes will auto-populate cells.

- To change the images shown in **Contact Sheet** mode, use the **Distribution** option in Image Options to control image replacement.

6. (Optional) From the left-hand pane, click the ▷ button beside **Image Options** for sizing and rotating images in cells:

- Enable **Fit image to cell** to make the image fit within the cell boundaries.

- Enable **Fill cell with image** to scale the image to fit all of the cell.

- Check **Rotate for best fit** to make portrait images fit cells of landscape orientation (and vice versa) to make maximum use of cell space.

7. (Optional) Check **Border** to add a border of a configurable width (use input box) and **Colour** (click the swatch to select colour from a dialog).

8. (Optional) To caption your images, check **Label** to add a Date, image Filename, or Sequence number under each image; select from the drop-down menu. For a combination of label formats, click **Modify...**, add tokens to assemble a sample name, then click **OK**; the drop-down menu changes to Custom. See Changing file names for more information.

9. Click | Print... |, or | Close | to save settings (but not print).

> To open additional images for printing, click | Add Images... |. Select a photo for addition then click **Open....** The image is added as a thumbnail to the gallery.

Sizing and rotating images in cells

▽ Image Options
◯ Fill cell with image   ◉ Fit image to cell
☐ Rotate for best fit

The Print dialog helps you size or rotate your image(s) to fit a cell(s) according to **Image Options** settings.

When the dialog is opened, the default settings above will be adopted. It's likely that some fine tuning might be needed, e.g. a portrait image may best be rotated to fit a cell of landscape orientation.

If further images are added from the image gallery, they will also adopt these settings. You can select an individual cell to affect the scaling or rotation on that cell only at a later time. To again apply a setting to all cells, first deselect a cell by clicking outside the grid.

Here's a visual breakdown of the different options.

Fit image to cell/Fill cell with image
These options toggle respectively between fitting the image to cell dimensions (it will scale the image width to cell width or image height to cell height) or making the image completely fill the cell, losing portions of the image from view.

Fit image to cell
enabled

Fill cell with image
enabled

Rotate for best fit
You can re-orient your image to fit cells using the **Rotate for best fit** check box—great for fitting a portrait image into landscape-oriented cells (and vice versa).

Rotate for best fit
unchecked

Rotate for best fit
checked

Cropping images in cells

If you're looking to be more specific about which areas of your image to print, you can crop your image instead of using the above Image Options. PhotoPlus supports some sophisticated cropping options, especially the ability to crop using the image or the image's cell dimensions.

To crop an image:

1. Select an image from the lower gallery and click Crop Image...

2. From the Crop Image dialog, choose an **Aspect Ratio** from the drop-down menu which dictates the proportions of your crop area grid: **Unconstrained** creates a grid which can be proportioned in any way; **Cell** matches to cell dimensions; **Image** maintains image dimensions; **Custom** uses a custom constrained ratio (e.g., a square) that you define yourself in the adjacent input boxes.

	Before	After
Unconstrained		
Cell		
Image (default)		

Custom
(e.g., 1.00 x 1.00 in)

3. Drag a crop area's corner to size your crop according to requirements, then move the grid around the image to choose the preferred image area to be cropped. To revert, click **Clear** to reset your crop grid.

4. Click **OK**.

If your image is already present in your layout then it will update automatically to reflect the new cropping applied. If it hasn't yet been used, the crop is still applied to the image in the image gallery.

 Cropping affects every instance of the image. Once applied, all images are updated.

Printing using colour separations

The Separations and Prepress options, shown for every mode, are used for professional printing with CMYK colour separations. This process is now a less popular printing method compared to electronic PDF publishing (using PDF/X1 compliance). See PhotoPlus help for more details.

Publishing a PDF file

PDF (Portable Document Format) is a cross-platform file format developed by Adobe. In a relatively short time, PDF has evolved into a worldwide standard for document distribution which works equally well for electronic or paper publishing. PDF documents are uniformly supported in the Windows, Macintosh, and UNIX® environments. Anyone with the free Adobe Acrobat® Reader can view or print out PDF files, either from within a Web browser window or directly—for example, when delivered over a network or on CD-ROM. PDF documents are compact—one-fifth the size of comparable HTML files—for faster transmission.

PDF works well as a medium for distributing standalone files. By letting people download an online PDF file, you can save yourself the trouble and expense of printing multiple copies! PDF is also used extensively for delivering files to professional printers. For the most part, print shops have adopted PDF artwork using **PDF/X** formats—more reliable than PostScript and expressly targeted for graphic arts and high quality reproduction. Several different "flavours" of PDF/X exist; PhotoPlus supports PDF/X-1 and PDF/X-1a.

To export a PhotoPlus picture as a PDF:

1. Choose **Publish as PDF...** from the **File** menu to display the **Publish PDF** dialog.

2. Set basic output options on the dialog's **General** tab (shown).

    • Checking **Fit to complete page** or **Fit to page width** to set the default page view when the PDF is opened in Acrobat Reader.

    • Checking **Preview PDF file in Acrobat** automatically opens the PDF in Acrobat after it's been created, so you can review it immediately. (If anything looks amiss, you'll need to fix the problems in the file and regenerate the PDF.)

    • If handing off a file to a professional printer, choose either "PDF X/1" or "PDF X/1a" in the **Compatibility** list as advised by your print partner (otherwise just use an Acrobat *X.0* option, where *X* is the version number).

• In the Colour Management section, the **Output colour space** setting should always be "CMYK" for professional printing; otherwise "RGB" is fine. Select the **Destination profile** recommended by your print partner.

• The **Prepress Marks** section lets you include printer marks in your PDF output (check an option to switch on). Use for professional printing.

3. Set security options (if any) on the **Security** tab.

• You can add password protection to keep the contents of your document away from unintended eyes, and/or lock certain capabilities to prevent unauthorized dissemination or changes. For example, you can specify **No document printing** to prevent paper reproduction of the publication's contents, or **No content copying** to help ensure your work can't be easily duplicated somewhere else. You can even enter a master password to give y`ou—and only you—the right to alter these security settings. (Just be sure to remember your password!)

4. Click **OK**.

Exporting to another file format

In many situations, you'll want to save a file to one of the standard graphics formats. In PhotoPlus, this is known as exporting.

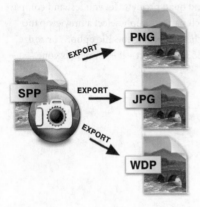

Exporting an image means converting it to a specified graphic file format other than the native PhotoPlus (.SPP) format. This flattens the image, removing layer information.

Only the .SPP and the Photoshop .PSD format preserves image information, such as multiple layers, masks, or image map data that would be lost in conversion to another format.

The Export process itself can be carried out by using either a standard file dialog where you can specify the path, name and format of the image file, or by using an Export Optimizer where you can additionally compare export previews for multiple file formats before export.

To export an image:

1. Choose **Export...** from the **File** menu.

2. The Export dialog appears, with the file's current base name shown. Change the base name if desired.

3. To open the Export Optimizer to fine-tune export settings, click **Optimizer** (see p. 201), then click **OK**.

4. Click **Save** in the **Export** dialog.

> The Export dialog includes additional options for use with Web images (see Slicing images and Creating image maps on p. 173 and p. 174).

You can also open the Export Optimizer first and (at your discretion) proceed to the exporting step after checking your settings. You can access the Export Optimizer at any time—not just at export time—to compare image quality using different settings (your settings are retained for each format).

The Export Optimizer consists of a left-hand preview display (single, dual, or quad) and a right-hand settings region, with additional View and Zoom buttons along the bottom of the dialog. Dual and quad previews let you test and compare between different export formats in each pane—simply select a preview pane and then test various quality settings, change format-specific options or resize before going ahead with your optimized file's export—it even retains your preferred settings for each format!

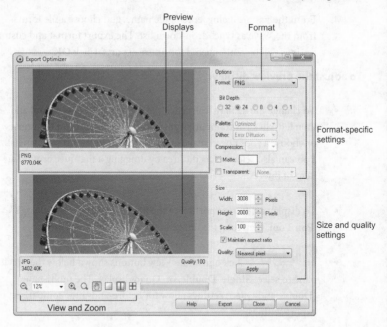

Preview Displays

Format

Format-specific settings

Size and quality settings

View and Zoom

To open the Export Optimizer:

1. Click ![icon] **Export Optimizer** on the **Standard** toolbar.

2. From the Export Optimizer dialog, use the **Options** section to specify the file **Format**, and format-specific options such as bit depth, dithering, palette, and compression. The **Size** section lets you scale, stretch, or squash the image, while setting an export Quality setting (e.g., a resampling method such as Bicubic).

3. Review your optimized image, and click ![Export] when you're happy with it.

The ![Close] button will instead abort the export but save any format-specific option changes made in the dialog.

4.   From the Export dialog, enter a file name, and choose a file format from the "Save as type" drop-down list. The export format and custom settings will be remembered for future exports. Click **OK**.

To adjust the preview display:

- To change the display scale, click the dialog's 🔍 **Zoom Tool** and then left-click (to zoom in), right-click (to zoom out) on the preview, or choose a zoom percentage in the lower left in the drop-down list. You can also select a specific area by dragging a marquee around an item of interest.

- To display a different portion of the image, first select the dialog's ✋ **Pan Tool**, then drag the image in the active preview pane.

- ⬜⬜⊞ Click one of the View buttons shown below the preview pane to select **Single**, **Double**, or **Quad** display. The multi-pane (Double and Quad) settings allow for before-and-after comparison of export settings.

To compare export settings:

1.   Set the preview display for either **Double** or **Quad** view (see above).

2.   Click one of the preview display panes to select it as the active pane.

3.   In the Options section, choose an export format and specific settings. Each time you make a new choice, the active pane updates to show the effect of filtering using the new settings, as well as the estimated file size.

4.   To compare settings, select a different display pane and repeat the process. The Export Optimizer lets you experiment freely and evaluate the results.

To revert back to a single pane, click ⬜ **Single**.

To proceed with exporting:

1. Make sure the active preview pane is using the settings you want to apply to the image.

2. Click the dialog's **Export** or **OK** button to display the Export dialog.

> ★ The Export Optimizer saves settings for particular formats according to the most recent update in the Options section. In other words, if you have two or more preview panes displaying the same file format, the settings for the last of them you click in will be those associated with exporting in that format.

To preview an image in your web browser:

- Choose **Preview in Browser...** from the **File** menu. PhotoPlus exports the image as a temporary file, then opens the file for preview in your web browser.

Sharing documents by email

The widespread availability of the Internet means that colleagues, family and friends are now only a quick email away. Higher line speeds via Broadband connections open up new opportunities for sharing documents in their native file format (.SPP) or as converted JPGs.

PhotoPlus lets you send your currently selected document to your standard email program (e.g., Outlook) for subsequent mailing. You can do this by choosing **Send...** from the **File** menu to display a dialog which sets the file type and image size restrictions.

After this, if the email program is not loaded, a Choose Profile dialog lets you select your email program, then a new email message is displayed with document attached. If already loaded, your email program automatically attaches your document to a new email message.

To complete the process, press the Send button (or equivalent) on your email program as for any other email message.

Setting the file type

To take advantage of better file compression you may want to convert your image to JPEG if not already in this format. The conversion would be suitable if your original document was in TIF format or was a very complex multi-layered SPP file.

From the above dialog, send the original SPP file by enabling the **Keep Original** radio button. To convert to JPEG and send as such, enable **Convert to JPEG**.

Setting your image size

PhotoPlus allows you to send any photo directly by email with an added file size limiter if necessary. This avoids sending excessively large files—this could affect your popularity!

Click the **Limit image dimensions to a maximum of** check box and select a suitable image resolution—this will be the new pixel height or width (the biggest pixel dimension of the original photo will be reduced to the new image size). Alternatively, keep original image dimensions by leaving the option unchecked.

 An Internet connection is required to email pictures.

11

Index

Notes

Notes